CASTLES

Written by Laura Buller

Illustrated by Robert Ball

DK

Penguin
Random
House

Author Laura Buller
Illustrator Robert Ball
Consultants Dr. Stuart Prior, Dr. Richard Nevell

Project editor Olivia Stanford
Senior art editor Elle Ward
Editorial assistant Abi Luscombe
Design assistant Katherine Marriott
US Senior editor Shannon Beatty
US Editor Margaret Parrish
Editorial assistance Abby Aitcheson, Sally Beets,
Katie Lawrence, James Mitchem
Design assistance Bettina Myklebust Stovne, Lucy Sims
Senior picture researcher Sumedha Chopra
Cartography Simon Mumford
DTP designer Vijay Kandwal
Jacket coordinator Issy Walsh
Jacket designer Elle Ward
Senior production editor Nikoleta Parasaki
Production controller Barbara Ossowska
Managing editor Jonathan Melmoth
Managing art editor Diane Peyton Jones
Publishing director Sarah Larter

First American Edition, 2020
Published in the United States by DK Publishing
1450 Broadway, Suite 801, New York, NY 10018

Text and design copyright © 2020 Dorling Kindersley Limited
Color illustrations © 2020 Robert Ball
DK, a Division of Penguin Random House LLC
20 21 22 23 24 10 9 8 7 6 5 4 3 2 1
001–317733–Sept/2020

A catalog record for this book
is available from the Library of Congress.
ISBN 978-1-4654-9855-7

DK books are available at special discounts when
purchased in bulk for sales promotions, premiums,
fund-raising, or educational use. For details, contact:
DK Publishing Special Markets,
1450 Broadway, Suite 801, New York, NY 10018
SpecialSales@dk.com

Printed and bound in China

For the curious
www.dk.com

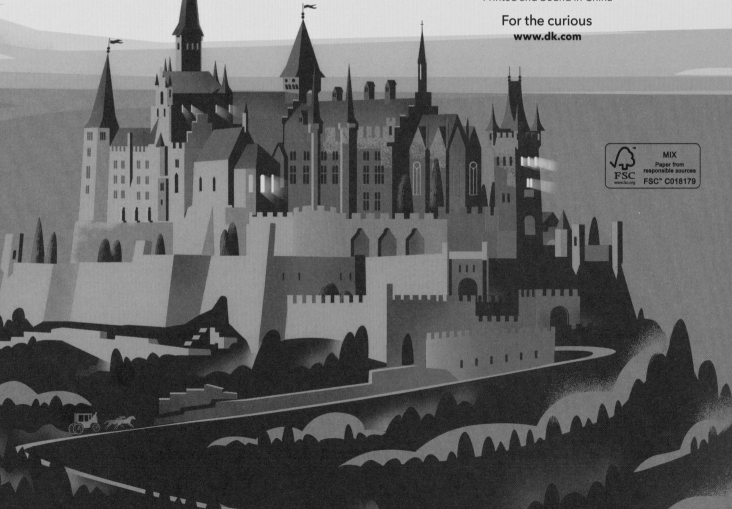

MIX
Paper from
responsible sources
FSC™ C018179

Contents

Travel through time and explore some of the world's most fascinating castles, starting with the 11th-century Hen Domen and moving right up to modern Hearst Castle.

In this book, the current-day countries are given for the location of each castle.

Nothe Fort, England

Fort

During wars, defensive buildings were needed to protect the lands around them and also to act as a base from which attacks could be launched. Forts were strong military buildings, but they weren't used as homes for nobles like castles were.

What is a castle?

Keep ----

Medieval castle

Castles have been built for hundreds of years, but perhaps the most familiar are those built in Europe toward the end of the Middle Ages. These medieval castles, such as Bodiam Castle in England, often have stone walls, tall towers, moats, and drawbridges.

The two main functions of a castle were to be a military stronghold and to be an impressive home for a monarch or noble. Many castles shared similar features, but there were no set rules for building one. Some were small wooden structures, and others were more like fortified towns. Confusingly, not all castles are known as castles—and some buildings that are known as castles are, in fact, not.

Palace

Palaces were built as grand, private residences for royal rulers or other high-ranking leaders. Although impressive, and often guarded, palaces were not built to be defensive structures. A palace would have struggled to withstand a long siege, unlike a castle.

Winter Palace, Russia

Battlements

Tower

Walls

Arrow slit

Moat

Bridge

Castles
through the ages

While the main reasons for building a castle or fort—to live in and fight from—did not change very much, building styles changed over time. New tools and materials made it easier to construct better and stronger fortresses. Castle designs also had to adapt to the development of new weapons and military strategies, to keep inhabitants safe.

Harbottle Castle, England

Motte and bailey

This type of castle was made of wood and featured a keep that sat on top of a steep hill called a motte. The area around it—the bailey—was enclosed by a wall.

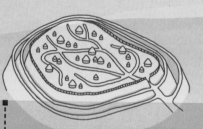

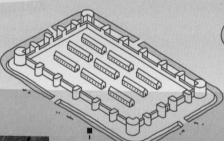

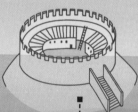

Maiden Hill Castle, England

Roman forts

When Roman soldiers moved to an area, they often built a fort to live in. These forts were usually rectangular, with strong stone walls. There were guarded gateways on each side.

Shell keeps

Timber motte and bailey castles could easily burn down, so castle builders came up with shell keeps. Stone walls were added to the tops of mottes to strengthen them.

Hardknott Fort, England

Burcht van Leiden, the Netherlands

Hill forts

Some of the first defenses for hilltop settlements were deep trenches dug into the ground. This left steep banks of soil behind. The trenches around these hill forts were hard to climb over.

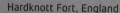

Château de Falaise, France

Starforts

A castle with round or square walls was hard to protect, since defenders could only see attackers right in front of them. Building castles in a star shape meant defenders could see other parts of the castle walls, too.

Goryōkaku Fort, Japan

Stone keeps

Over time, stone castles became more common. Not only were they sturdier and longer-lasting, but they also looked imposing. A stone keep kept the ruling family in comfort and was also harder to destroy.

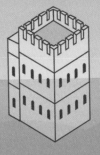

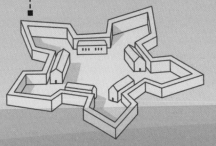

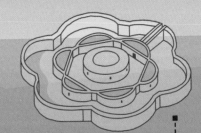

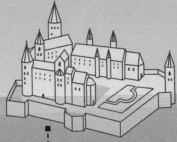

Fairy-tale castles

While most castles were fortresses, designed for defense, some were constructed simply to show the wealth and power of the ruling family. No expense was spared on creating these fantastical homes.

Hohenschwangau Castle, Germany

Caerphilly Castle, Wales

Concentric castles

Having one wall is good, but having two is even better. A concentric castle featured rings of defenses—often a high inner wall and a low outer wall. A moat added another layer of protection.

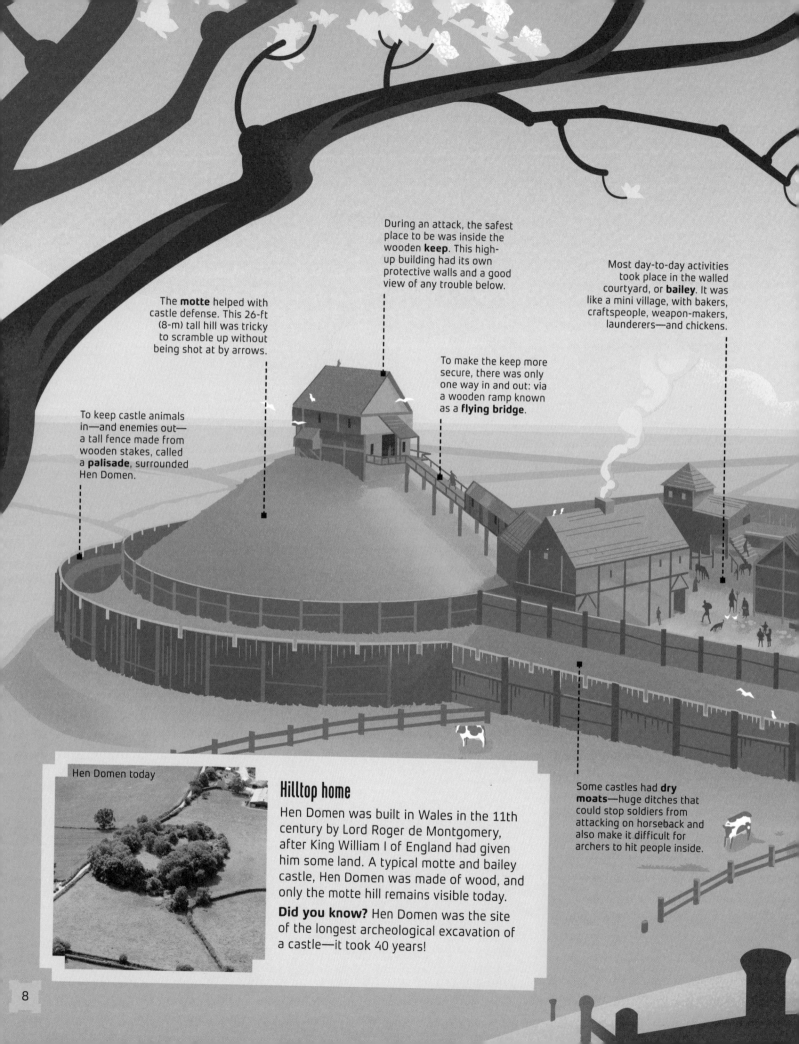

During an attack, the safest place to be was inside the wooden **keep**. This high-up building had its own protective walls and a good view of any trouble below.

The **motte** helped with castle defense. This 26-ft (8-m) tall hill was tricky to scramble up without being shot at by arrows.

Most day-to-day activities took place in the walled courtyard, or **bailey**. It was like a mini village, with bakers, craftspeople, weapon-makers, launderers—and chickens.

To make the keep more secure, there was only one way in and out: via a wooden ramp known as a **flying bridge**.

To keep castle animals in—and enemies out—a tall fence made from wooden stakes, called a **palisade**, surrounded Hen Domen.

Hen Domen today

Hilltop home

Hen Domen was built in Wales in the 11th century by Lord Roger de Montgomery, after King William I of England had given him some land. A typical motte and bailey castle, Hen Domen was made of wood, and only the motte hill remains visible today.

Did you know? Hen Domen was the site of the longest archeological excavation of a castle—it took 40 years!

Some castles had **dry moats**—huge ditches that could stop soldiers from attacking on horseback and also make it difficult for archers to hit people inside.

Hen Domen

Wales, April 1071

Plan of Hen Domen, 1071

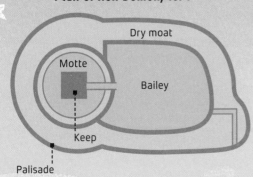

On an early spring morning in Wales, people were already bustling about the castle of Hen Domen. From lighting fires to tending the fields, there was plenty to do. Hen Domen's keep sat high on a huge hill of piled-up soil called a motte, next to a courtyard enclosed by a protective outer wall—the bailey. Motte and bailey castles were formidable, but not too challenging to build. Hen Domen was newly constructed, so craftspeople were busy creating homes for the new residents.

Hen Domen translated from Welsh means "old mound."

The fewer **entrances** to guard, the safer the castle residents would be. Only specific people were allowed inside the castle grounds.

Finding a site

First, the location of the castle must be found, which can be tricky if the castle has disappeared. Archeologists look at written records, maps, and even use 3-D laser imaging to find hidden features. Sometimes all that can be seen above ground are defensive ditches.

Digging

Once the site is identified and permission is given, digging can begin. The archeologists look for everything from the tiniest objects to the remains of walls and buildings. As the team members dig down, they are digging further back in time.

Barbury Castle, England

Excavations

hy do some castles disappear? Some are destroyed in wars. Others are neglected and fall into ruin or may have been torn down to make way for newer buildings. Older castles made from wood might have rotted away completely. So how do we know about them? Archeologists excavate a castle's remains and help uncover its hidden history—secrets often buried deep underground.

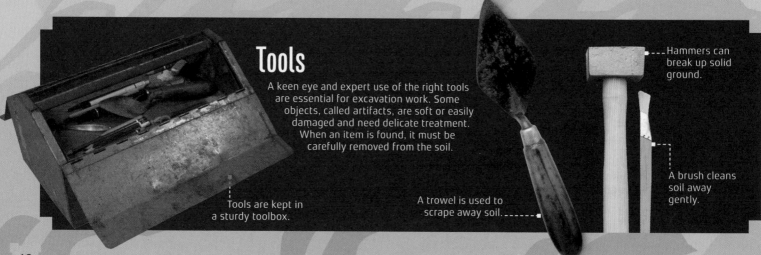

Tools

A keen eye and expert use of the right tools are essential for excavation work. Some objects, called artifacts, are soft or easily damaged and need delicate treatment. When an item is found, it must be carefully removed from the soil.

Hammers can break up solid ground.

A brush cleans soil away gently.

Tools are kept in a sturdy toolbox.

A trowel is used to scrape away soil.

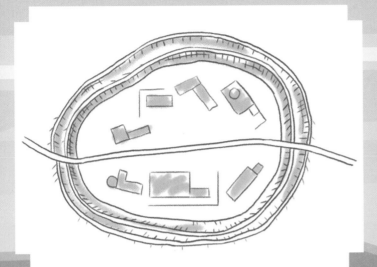

Drawing

It is important to record when and where everything is found. Photographs are taken and drawings made of the site to build the dig record. This helps create a picture of the castle and how it was used.

Sorting artifacts

Each object found is given a number to identify it. Sometimes items are put in bags and carefully labeled for study after the excavation is finished. They can also be sent off for scientific dating or other types of analysis in a lab.

Reconstruction of a motte and bailey castle

Reconstructing

After many months of study and research, and a lot of digging, specialists can create a reconstruction of the castle. These models, which can be physical or on a computer, show how a castle would have looked. A virtual walk-through of a castle is the next best thing to time travel.

Oxford Castle

England, September 1142

One of the castle's oldest buildings, **St. George's Tower** was rectangular in shape but got thinner near the top to help stop it from toppling over. It made for a good watchtower.

The **motte** was the first part of the castle that was built. It was 59 ft (18 m) tall and topped with a keep.

St. George's Chapel was built around 1074. A Welsh monk who lived here wrote stories about legendary King Arthur.

The path of a stream running from the Thames River was changed to flow around the castle and fill the **moat**.

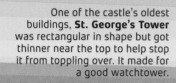

Oxford Castle today

Norman construction

Oxford Castle was built in the 11th century by Robert D'Oyly on the orders of King William I of England. Initially a motte and bailey castle, it was rebuilt in stone to strengthen it. Today, the remains of the castle are found at the heart of the city of Oxford.

Did you know? The castle was used as a prison from the 13th century right up until 1966.

It was harvesttime at Oxford Castle, and the farmers, butchers, and fishermen were working to stock up the pantries for winter. More importantly, they had a famous guest staying in the castle—Empress Matilda. She was the rightful queen and had been battling her cousin, Stephen, for the crown of England. Many nobles didn't think a woman could rule, but Matilda was determined to claim the throne that had belonged to her father, King Henry I. Unfortunately for her, Stephen had many supporters, and his army was approaching to try and trap her.

St. George's Tower was built long before Oxford Castle, but was incorporated into the bailey walls.

Stephen's **army** was on its way to besiege the castle.

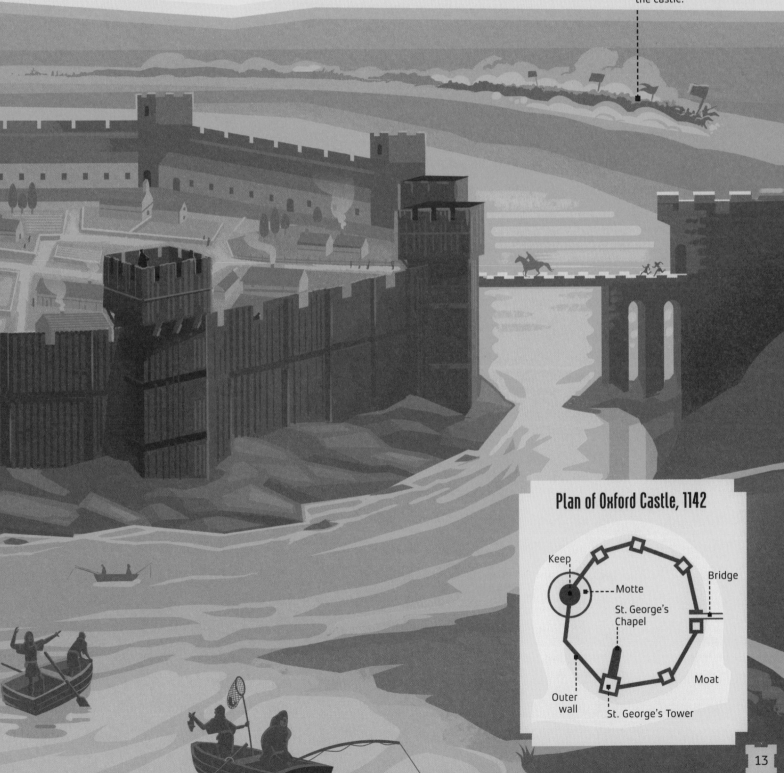

Plan of Oxford Castle, 1142

Keep

Motte

St. George's Chapel

Bridge

Moat

Outer wall

St. George's Tower

Matilda escaped to the river from **St. George's Tower** to make her daring dash.

Escape on ice

Stephen hoped to end the battle for the crown by capturing Empress Matilda, but she managed a crafty escape. She scaled the castle walls and silently skated across the frozen river to safety. The next day, the residents of the castle surrendered.

Stephen's **soldiers** were left confused when they found out that Matilda had escaped.

A frosty flight

Oxford Castle, December 1142

By winter, Stephen's army had surrounded Oxford Castle and trapped Empress Matilda inside. Matilda and her surviving soldiers were huddled within the thick walls of St. George's Tower watching their supplies dwindle by the day. However, the newly frozen river gave them an idea for a risky but clever escape plan. In the dead of night, the empress and three of her closest knights sneaked out of the castle walls.

Matilda dressed in a **white cloak** to help her stay hidden in the snow.

The **river** was frozen over, so the empress could skate across to freedom.

15

Medieval Society

Society during the medieval period was very structured, and it was not easy to move between its levels. Imagine a pyramid with a king or queen at the top, the nobles below, and the peasants at the bottom. This was known as the feudal system. The king or queen ruled over almost every aspect of life, and, in turn, everyone worked for the monarch.

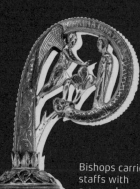

A **crown** worn by a monarch was a symbol of power.

Bishops carried staffs with a curved end called **croziers**.

Knights carried weapons—such as **daggers**—for protection.

Craftspeople made woolen yarn using a **spindle**.

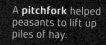

A **pitchfork** helped peasants to lift up piles of hay.

Monarch

Royal rule was absolute. The king or queen had the power to make almost every decision for the country. They created laws, declared or ended wars, owned the land, and were responsible for their citizens.

Lords, ladies, and bishops

Nobles called lords and ladies served the king in return for large areas of land. They often lived in castles. Religion played an important role in medieval society, and bishops were high-ranking members of the Church who could also live in castles.

Japanese society

For 250 years, starting in the 17th century, Japan also had a feudal system. At the top, there was an emperor instead of a monarch. Next was the shogun, who controlled the nobles, called daimyos. The first shogun was Tokugawa Ieyasu.

Tokugawa Ieyasu

Clergy and knights

Lower-ranking members of the clergy, such as priests and nuns, reported to the bishops. Unlike many people, most of the clergy could read and write. A knight was devoted to his lord or lady and could be called up to fight for them.

Craftspeople and bailiffs

Skilled craftspeople could earn money and status by making goods, such as armor, shoes, or candles. Bailiffs helped their lord or lady to manage their lands or worked in courts of law.

Servants and peasants

The majority of people were peasants. Nobles gave peasants small farms in return for money and a portion of the food they produced. Some peasants worked as servants for people in a higher class.

Kerak Castle

Jordan, November 1183

Kerak Castle was a mighty Crusader stronghold. The castle was imposing, but Saladin, the Sultan of Egypt and Syria, was set on besieging it because the castle's ruler, Raynald of Châtillon, had made attacks on surrounding cities. However, at that moment, an important wedding was taking place. Raynald's heir, Humphrey IV of Toron, was to marry Isabella of Jerusalem. Nothing would stop Saladin, but he did direct his weapons away from the newlyweds' rooms. Eventually, supporting forces came to Raynald's aid and Saladin retreated.

Raynald executed prisoners by fitting boxes on their heads and throwing them over the castle walls.

The castle sat on a craggy cliffside and had a **glacis**—a steep stone wall running around the bottom of the outer walls that was difficult for attackers to climb.

According to legend, the defenders sent a gift of food and wine to **Saladin** to persuade him not to attack the wedding.

Kerak Castle today

Clifftop castle

Kerak was constructed in central Jordan in the 12th century by King Fulk of Jerusalem. The Sultan of Egypt, Baibars, expanded the defenses in the 13th century, but in the 19th century much of the castle was destroyed.

Did you know? Kerak is a "spur castle," meaning it is built on a hill, or spur, making it easier to defend.

Dry moat

Cistern

Lower courtyard

Keep

Upper courtyard

Dry moat

Glacis

Entrance

Church

The **rooms** of the newly married Princess Isabella and Humphrey IV were spared from the attack.

A deep **dry moat** separated the castle from the gatehouse. Over time, it was made wider. Even without water, it could slow down attackers.

Saladin's army brought siege weapons, such as **trebuchets**, to try to damage the castle walls.

Medieval banquet

Hosting a lavish banquet was one way the ruler of a castle could show off to guests. However, it was the cooks who did all the hard work. With no electricity and far fewer ingredients than are available today, they created all sorts of dishes from produce that could be found locally. Banquets could last for hours, with entertainment between the various courses.

Fruit

Fresh fruit, such as apples and grapes, were grown in kitchen gardens. Fruit was also made into cold soups, stewed in wine and spices, baked, or candied.

Pig's head

With an apple between its jaws and garnished with fruit and herbs, a pig's head was a real delicacy. Other meats served might include poultry, beef, or lamb.

Beer

Beer, or ale, was made from wheat, barley, or oats. Water was often unsafe to drink so beer was drunk instead. Some beer was brewed by women known as alewives.

Apple pie

An apple pie might contain raisins and spices, but most recipes did not contain sugar, so pies tasted sharp. The crust was not usually eaten, it was just a container.

Royal feast

Kings or queens would sometimes visit nobles in their castles, and a banquet fit for royalty would be needed. Unlike peasants, the rich ate expensive food, such as meat, and some nobles spent all their money preparing for such a feast!

Pheasant

Castle cooks often made elaborate dishes to surprise and amaze the guests. A roasted pheasant, for example, might be adorned with its own tail feathers.

Peppercorns

Nutmeg

Cinnamon

Pottage

A thick soup made from meats, grains, and vegetables, pottage was a common dish for both rich and poor. Turnips, leeks, cabbage, parsnips, onions, oats, or barley might be added.

Bread plate

Guests put their food on stale bread "plates" called trenchers. Forks didn't exist yet, so people used a knife or their fingers to eat.

Cheese

Cheese was popular because it lasted a long time. Milk would turn bad quickly without a place to keep it cool, so it was made into cheese.

Spices

Spices were some of the most expensive ingredients. Cinnamon, pepper, nutmeg, and cloves had to be shipped from abroad.

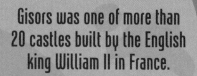

Gisors was one of more than 20 castles built by the English king William II in France.

The castle was mostly a fortress, but it also served as a home for visiting royalty. **Chambers** in the keep provided a safe place to stay.

In the 12th century, Henry I of England replaced the wooden **keep** with a much stronger and longer-lasting octagonal stone one.

A low wall circled the keep. It was called a **chemise**—French for "skirt." The chemise added an extra layer of defense to the castle.

England in France

In the 11th century, King William II ordered Gisors to be built to protect English lands in France. Henry I and Henry II added stone fortifications, but the castle was repeatedly captured and eventually became part of France.

Did you know? The Knights Templar, a group of Christian knights, were rumored to have buried treasure in Gisors' motte, but it has never been found.

Château de Gisors today

22

Château de Gisors

France, January 1193

Plan of Château de Gisors, 1193

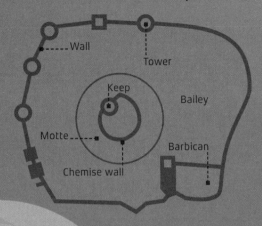

Wall

Tower

Keep

Bailey

Motte

Barbican

Chemise wall

Perched high on a motte, Château de Gisors had a commanding view of the surrounding countryside. It was built in France, in lands owned by the English. Unfortunately for them, their king—Richard I—had been captured abroad. Without their leader, the soldiers inside were very worried. Gisors was a key castle that the French king, Phillip II, desperately wanted to capture. They were right to be concerned—it wasn't long before Philip attacked and took over the castle.

The first part of the castle to be built, the **motte**, was about 49 ft (15 m) high.

Gisors was on the border between the lands controlled by England and France. **Soldiers** patrolled its grounds day and night to watch out for attacks.

Château Gaillard

France, August 1203

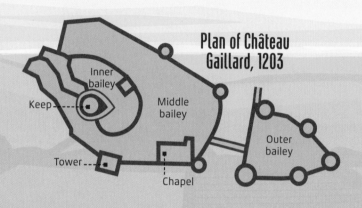

Plan of Château Gaillard, 1203

Inner bailey

Keep

Tower

Middle bailey

Chapel

Outer bailey

Towers gave castle defenders a clear view of their surroundings and of enemies approaching.

Thick stone **walls** had openings where human waste from the latrines emptied out.

The castle had **steep cliffs** beside it that led to the river below, making it almost impossible to attack.

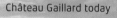
Château Gaillard today

Riverside resistance

King Richard I built Château Gaillard in under two years, between 1196 and 1198, to protect the then English region of Normandy, France. Control of the castle switched between England and France many times, but from the 15th century, it was gradually abandoned.

Did you know? In 1314, two future queens of France were kept prisoner in Gaillard's underground cells, and had their heads shaved!

The summer sun warmed the French countryside of Normandy, and the Seine River rippled beneath the towering walls of Château Gaillard. Built by King Richard I to defend English land in France, the castle was now ruled by his brother, King John. However, something was stirring. The French army was on the march. As the soldiers drew close to the walled town of Les Andelys, the townspeople panicked. It was an attack! Quick as they could, they rushed for the safety of the castle.

The **French army** was determined to take over the castle and surrounding lands, so they attacked the townspeople first, then besieged the castle.

The **Seine River** was used as a transportation route and ran 295 ft (90 m) below the castle through the Seine Valley.

Château Gaillard had strong **river defenses**, including a tower on a small island and dams blocking the waterway, to help protect the castle from an enemy attack on water.

If the Statue of Liberty stood in Les Andelys, the top would only just reach the level of Château Gaillard.

A small walled town on the riverside near the castle, called **Les Andelys**, was the site of the first attack by the French.

Richard the Lionheart

King Richard I of England earned his nickname "Lionheart" through his bravery in battle. His father gave him land in France, and Richard built Château Gaillard to protect it. He was rumored to have designed the castle himself. His brother King John I succeeded him.

Under siege

Château Gaillard, March 1204

Six months later, the sun had given way to winter's chill, and the French army had surrounded the castle. The English townspeople were safe within its walls, yet the same defenses that kept the French out also stopped supplies from getting in. King John had tried to rescue the castle, but failed. The English fought off attack after attack, but then the French found a way into the castle—through a latrine, or toilet chute!

The soldiers used **ladders** to try to scale the walls to get into the castle.

French soldiers cut off escape routes and kept the castle defenders trapped inside until supplies were close to running out.

The end of the attack

After the soldiers managed to sneak inside the castle through the latrine, they let the rest of the French army in. The English were overwhelmed, and the castle surrendered. The loss of Château Gaillard was a blow to King John and led to the English being driven out of Normandy.

Toilets in castles were often tiny rooms built into the castle walls. A wooden bench with a hole in the middle sat over the chute.

A handful of soldiers **climbed up** the smelly toilet chute.

Once the defending soldiers heard the enemy inside the castle, they lit **fires** to try to get them to retreat.

Some sneaky soldiers got into a **toilet chute** through an opening at the bottom where waste poured out.

Ballista

The ballista was a supersized crossbow. This device, first used by the ancient Greeks in around 400 BCE, could sling heavy objects a long way.

Two twisted **coils of rope** held the arms of the ballista, storing the energy to launch the missile.

A rope was pulled back to shoot a **missile**, such as an arrowlike bolt or a rock.

The ballista's arms were held by twisted coils of rope. When the missile was pulled back, the arms stored energy that, when released, launched the **projectile** with a giant snap!

Siege weapons

Ladders inside the tower let the soldiers get right to the top.

Siege tower

Castle walls too tall? Build a siege tower. This wooden structure gave shelter to attackers who hid inside while it was pushed right up against the castle.

Wheels allowed the attackers to roll the tower around easily.

Once pushed up against the castle walls, a **door** would drop down at the top of the tower to allow the attackers out and over the castle walls.

Battering ram

If attackers couldn't climb over or dig under castle walls, one option was to try to break through the castle door with a battering ram.

Wheels allowed soldiers to get more force behind the ram.

A **heavy log** was suspended by chains or ropes, so it could be swung back and forth to batter down even the heaviest wooden door.

Crash! Bam! Boom! Mighty machines called siege weapons were used to attack castles. Some were used to break down walls, while others were used to let attackers inside. Even though these devices look powerful, they were not always very effective. Reloading the weapons could be slow, and targets were not always easy to hit. Also, castles were built for defense, with their tall, strong walls.

Missiles included rounded rocks and sticky tar—even dead animals, beehives, or human heads were used.

Trebuchet

This super slingshot could throw heavy rocks or other missiles over castle walls or straight at them to try to break them down.

The trebuchet worked when a **weight** dropped and pulled one end of a beam down. This swung the other end of the beam up, launching the projectile into the air with great force and speed.

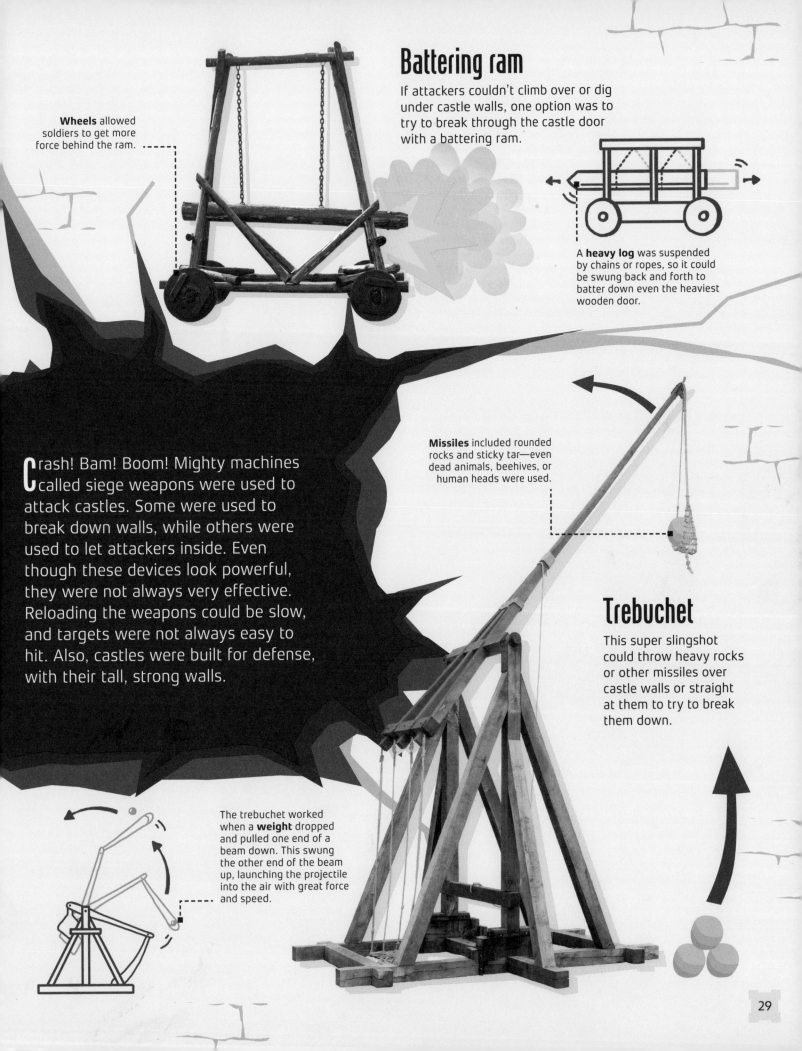

The ring wall around the city was topped with toothlike structures called **crenellations**. These gave archers a gap to shoot arrows through before they ducked behind the wall for safety.

Lookouts kept watch from many tall, semicircular **towers** along the city walls.

To protect the nobles, a castle fortress was built within Carcassonne called **Château Comtal**. This was the last defense of the castle. Within the château, the nobles would meet and discuss everything that was happening inside, and outside, the castle walls.

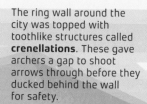

Carcassonne

France, August 1209

The winding walls and tall towers of the fortress city of Carcassonne were baking in the midday heat, but there was a nervous chill in the air. Carcassonne's strategic location had made the city a target for invaders time and again. The lord of the citadel, Raymond-Roger de Trencavel, was about to become the next target of a Crusade against his citizens. A tower guardsman noticed something as he scanned the horizon. He squinted in the bright summer sun. Was there an army in the distance?

Plan of Carcassonne, 1209

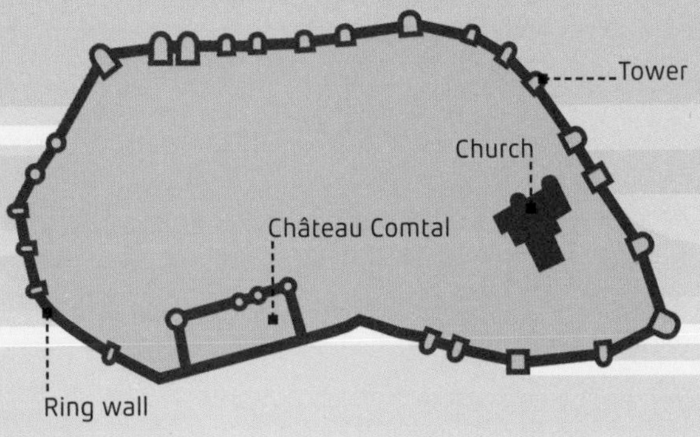
Tower
Church
Château Comtal
Ring wall

The ring wall surrounding Carcassonne was more than half a mile (1 km) long.

Defenders of the city patrolled its **ramparts**—narrow pathways just behind the crenellations. These gave them a bird's-eye view of the city surroundings.

Carcassonne today

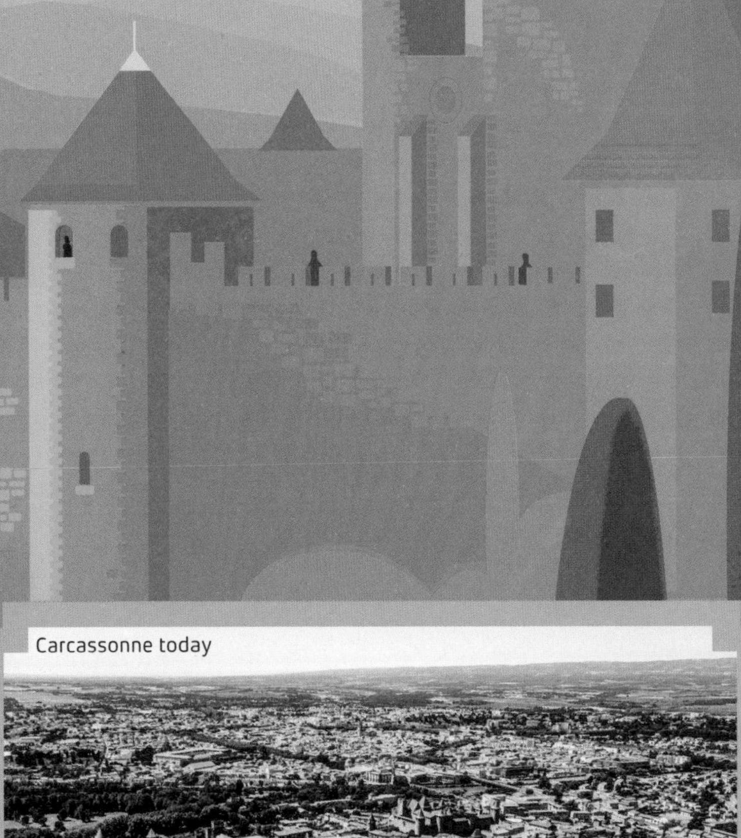

Walled city

Carcassonne began as a fortified settlement constructed by the Romans in around 100 BCE named Carcaso. It was expanded over hundreds of years, including the addition of a second ring wall in the 13th century. By the 19th century, Carcassonne had fallen into disrepair, but it was restored and is now a popular tourist attraction.

Did you know? In the 20th century, a Roman-style theater was built inside the city walls.

Hidden inside **turrets**, Carcassonne's defenders shot arrows at the attackers or launched projectiles down on them.

Fire was a formidable weapon. During the siege, the main water supply was cut off, so it was very hard to stop the flames from causing serious damage.

To get through the walls of the city, the invaders built a **siege tower**. The attackers climbed it to reach the ramparts.

The giant **cat** was a shelter put against the fortress to protect attackers while they battered a hole in the walls. Like their namesake, some cats had clawlike arms to dig through the stones.

Archers hid behind tall **shields**. These could be propped up to protect the archers so that they could safely reload their bows.

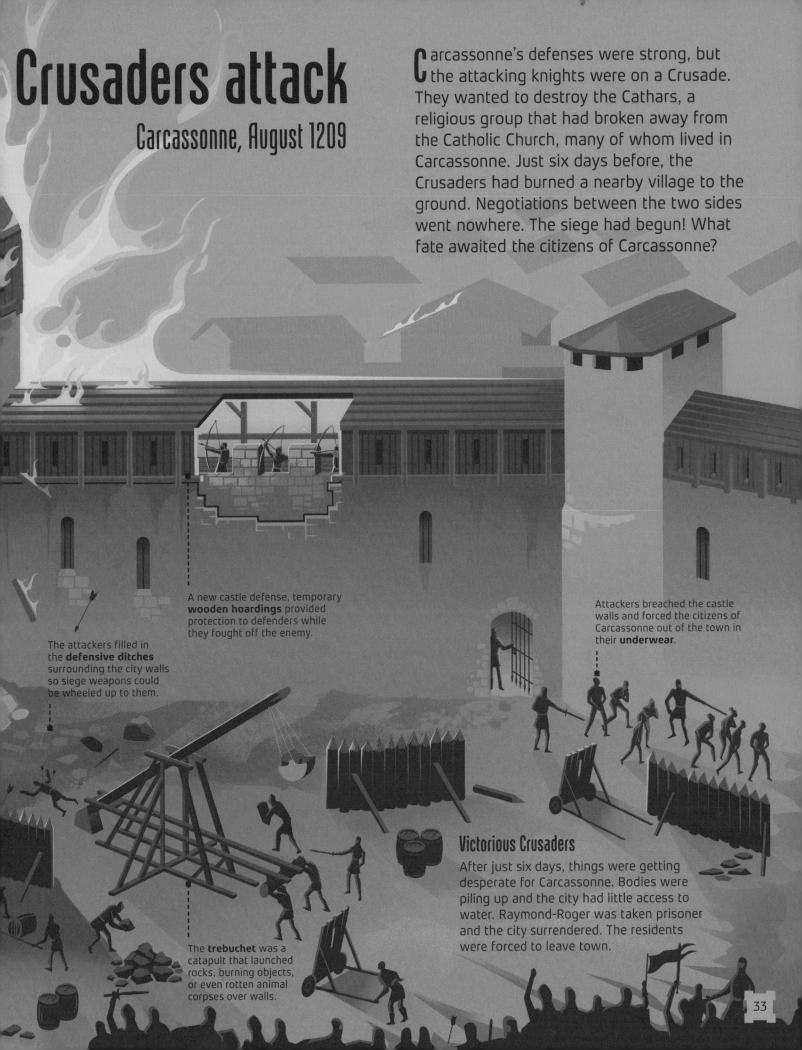

Crusaders attack
Carcassonne, August 1209

Carcassonne's defenses were strong, but the attacking knights were on a Crusade. They wanted to destroy the Cathars, a religious group that had broken away from the Catholic Church, many of whom lived in Carcassonne. Just six days before, the Crusaders had burned a nearby village to the ground. Negotiations between the two sides went nowhere. The siege had begun! What fate awaited the citizens of Carcassonne?

A new castle defense, temporary **wooden hoardings** provided protection to defenders while they fought off the enemy.

Attackers breached the castle walls and forced the citizens of Carcassonne out of the town in their **underwear**.

The attackers filled in the **defensive ditches** surrounding the city walls so siege weapons could be wheeled up to them.

Victorious Crusaders

After just six days, things were getting desperate for Carcassonne. Bodies were piling up and the city had little access to water. Raymond-Roger was taken prisoner and the city surrendered. The residents were forced to leave town.

The **trebuchet** was a catapult that launched rocks, burning objects, or even rotten animal corpses over walls.

Butler

Castle kitchens had a pantry for bread and other food, as well as a buttery for storing wine and beer. The butler was in charge of the buttery—an important job because some of its contents were very expensive.

Castle jobs

Running a castle came with a huge list of jobs. Some household staff lived in the castle itself, while others lived in cottages within the castle grounds. There were plenty of specialized workers, such as armorers, chandlers, cooks, butlers—even rat catchers. The castle steward, together with the the lady of the castle, made sure that all the necessary jobs got done.

Rat catcher

Pesky rats ate the castle's food supply and carried dangerous diseases. A rat catcher, well regarded in the castle, captured the pests with rat traps.

Cook

The kitchens of the castle were overseen by the cooks. There were many different types of cook—head cooks, roasting cooks, soup cooks, sauce cooks, and supply cooks in charge of the pantry.

Armorer

One of the most skilled jobs in the castle was making and taking care of the custom-made suits of armor. The armorer used his skills to hammer and weld the suit together, then adjusting it to fit.

Chandler

Stone walls and small windows made the rooms of a castle very dark, and candles were the main source of light. The chandler was in charge of making candles and keeping an eye on the supply.

The armorer used a **hammer** to bash and bend the metal to the right shape.

An **anvil** is a metal block that armor was shaped on.

Toilet cleaner

Castle toilets were very basic. People sat on a wooden plank or slab of stone with a hole in it, and their waste fell into the moat or into a pit dug in the ground. The terrible smell meant that every so often the toilet cleaner had to empty out the pit.

At your service

The lord and his family had servants to help them with all sorts of everyday tasks. Household workers served food, helped nobles to dress, and emptied chamberpots—a pot kept in a bedroom for use as a toilet in the night.

Wartburg Castle

Germany, February 1522

Rising from the forest on a rocky cliff some 722 ft (220 m) above the city of Eisenach, Wartburg Castle was host to many important visitors. Guests and residents of Wartburg included St. Elisabeth of Hungary, who built a hospital where she cared for the sick, German composer Richard Wagner, who wrote an opera about a singing contest held there, and a monk named Martin Luther. In 1552, Luther, who had decided to challenge the Catholic Church, was hiding in the castle under a fake name.

South tower

Knights' rooms

Watchtower

Palas

Elisabethengang

Drawbridge

Plan of Wartburg Castle, 1522

The **Elisabethengang** was a covered walkway that ran from the gateway to the palas. It was added sometime around the 14th–15th century.

The **palas** contained a banquet room, knights' hall, and a singers' hall.

Forest fortress

Wartburg Castle dates back to the 11th century. It was built in central Germany by Count Louis the Springer to defend the borders of his lands. In the 14th century, much of the castle was rebuilt after a lightning strike, and after years of neglect the castle was restored again in the 20th century.

Did you know? Count Louis had soil from his own property dug up and moved to Wartburg's site so that he could claim the new castle was on his own land, even though it wasn't.

Wartburg Castle today

While in Wartburg, Martin Luther called himself "Knight George" and grew a beard as a disguise.

Martin Luther

Martin Luther was a monk who helped start a movement called the Reformation, in protest against the power and control of the Catholic Church. This angered many people and Luther hid in Wartburg. Here, he secretly worked on translating the Bible into German from Ancient Greek so ordinary people could read and understand its words.

Martin Luther worked in a simple set of rooms during his time in hiding at the castle. Between 1521 and 1522, he worked at his desk to translate the Bible.

The fortified **barbican** over the castle gate helped to prevent attackers from storming the castle.

To enter the castle, visitors crossed one of the oldest parts of the castle, a **drawbridge** across the moat.

Festsaal

This massive room, also known as the Festival Hall, runs the length of the top floor of the palas. It was used for large banquets, but today it hosts live music. The Festsaal partly inspired the Singers' Hall in Neuschwanstein Castle.

Elisabeth Kemenate

In the 13th century, Elisabeth of Hungary lived at the castle. In the 20th century, mosaics made from glass, shell, and gold were added to this room to tell the story of her life, especially her work caring for the sick.

Rittersaal

The Rittersaal, or Knights' Hall, is found in the palas. Stone columns support its arched ceilings. A large fireplace in the corner meant this room could be made warm easily and meals could be eaten here.

Prince's bedroom

This room has been restored to show what a grand royal bedroom would have looked like. The wooden bed and table were finely carved, and the walls and ceilings were richly decorated.

Inside
Wartburg Castle

In the 19th century, the lady of Wartburg Castle, Grand Duchess Maria Pavlovna, began collecting pieces to start a museum at the castle. Today, the collection contains more than 9,000 objects and artworks. In the 20th century, the castle was restored, and today many people visit to learn about the building's history and to see the treasures in the museum. Even the room where Martin Luther worked is now open for visitors to see.

Lutherstube

This room is where Martin Luther worked. The space was plain and simple, with a desk, chair, and green-tiled heater. The one unusual piece of furniture was his footstool—made from a bone from the back of a whale!

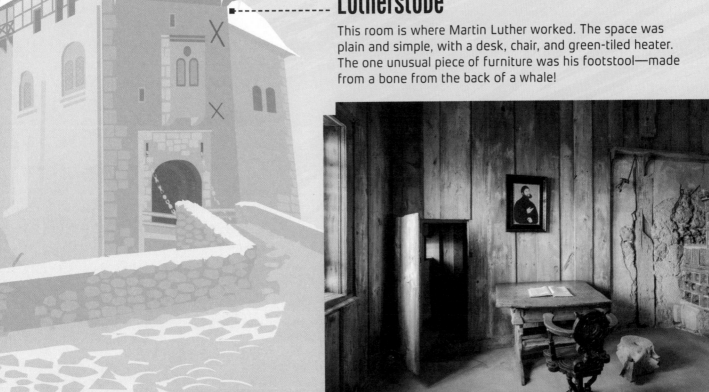

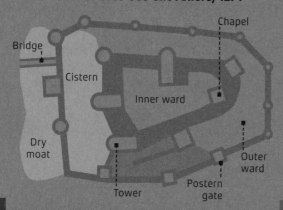

Plan of Crac des Chevaliers, 1271

Bridge

Cistern

Chapel

Inner ward

Dry moat

Tower

Postern gate

Outer ward

Some defensive **towers** were not square but slightly rounded, like the letter D. This design was useful because attackers could not lean a siege engine against the rounded front.

In 1170, an earthquake crumbled the original chapel.

In the 13th century, an outer ring **wall** was built surrounding the existing inner wall.

The southwest tower was damaged during the **siege**.

A water-filled ditch, called a **cistern**, on the south side of the castle divided the inner and outer walls. It was a handy water supply in a siege as well as a defensive obstacle.

Baibars' army built **mangonels**, a sort of catapult, to launch rocks at the castle walls.

Attackers hoping to storm the castle gates had to pass through a long, twisting **corridor**. Unfortunately for them, the ceiling was dotted with gaps and holes for dropping down boulders or spears.

Crac des Chevaliers

Syria, March 1271

The castle's inner walls were built around a **courtyard**. Towers topped the limestone ring, and three well-defended entrances kept the castle secure.

R ain brought a temporary halt to the fierce battle raging at Crac de Chevaliers. Warriors led by the Sultan of Egypt, Baibars, had launched an attack on the Knights Hospitaller inside the castle. This Crusader fortress had withstood many attacks and the local people had taken refuge inside its walls. However, the outer wall soon fell and a forged letter from Baibars to the knights, supposedly from their commander, tricked them into surrendering.

The **outer ward** provided protection for the surrounding population during the attack.

Crac des Chevaliers today

Crusader castle

Constructed by the emir, or king, Shibl ad-Dawla Nasr of Aleppo, in Syria in the 11th century, the original castle was taken over by the Knights Hospitaller in the 12th century. After earthquake damage to the building, the castle as it looks today was created in the 13th century.

Did you know? The huge storerooms of the castle could hold food and supplies to last five years.

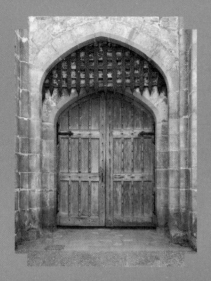

Portcullis

To block off a castle entrance, a heavy grate, called a portcullis, could be slid in front of a doorway. Portcullises were usually made of wood that was sometimes covered with a layer of iron.

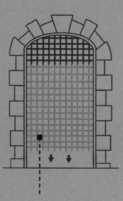

Arrows could be fired through the holes in the portcullis.

Moat

A moat was a trench surrounding a castle, often filled with water. Moats made tunneling under the castle or rolling weapons up to its walls impossible.

Attackers would have to wade or swim through a moat to reach the castle.

Castle defenses

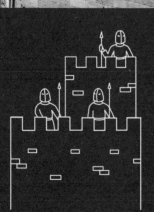

Crenellations

Many castle walls were topped by toothlike raised sections with gaps in between, known as crenellations. Soldiers could hide out of sight behind the "teeth," called merlons, then dash out to release an arrow through the gaps, the crenels, in an attack.

Murder holes

These were openings in the ceiling above an entrance to the castle. Castle defenders pushed heavy rocks or poured red-hot sand through them to rain down on attackers.

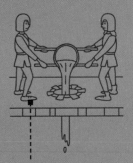

Defenders could attack enemies safely from a room above the gate.

Choosing a good defensive site for a castle, such as on high ground, made a fortress harder to attack, and tall, thick walls kept out most enemies. However, castle builders had several tricks to make fortresses extra secure. These defensive structures changed over time as new weapons were invented, and a well-built castle became almost impossible to break into.

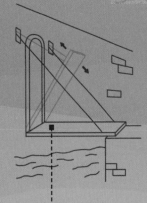

Drawbridge

A castle's entrance was often the most difficult spot to defend. A drawbridge was a section of the bridge over a moat that could be hoisted up to seal the gateway.

Raising the **drawbridge** meant that the moat completely circled a castle.

Crenellations made the battlements easier to defend.

Foundations

In addition to being built on high ground, some castles had tall, steep-sloped foundations, called glacis. These were tricky to scramble up and they also made tunneling in from underneath the castle walls very difficult.

Japanese castles had curved stone foundations called **musha-gaeshi**.

Windsor Castle

England, July 1278

The bailey to the west of the Round Tower was known as the **lower ward**. It was always full of people, whether they were working, tending to their animals, or going to church.

Windsor's first chapel was the **Chapel of St. Edward the Confessor**. It was constructed by Henry III in the early 13th century.

The castle site overlooking the **Thames River** helped to secure the western river route to London.

The thick **stone walls** were added in the 12th century to replace earlier wooden ones.

A **dry moat** was created as workers dug up the chalky soil to build the tall motte. The moat made it tricky for invaders to get to the castle walls.

Horses, both for riding and for pulling carriages, lived in the castle **stables**, alongside places for the grooms to sleep, food stores, and equipment rooms.

The lower ward was always busy, with lots of people entering and exiting via the main **entrance**.

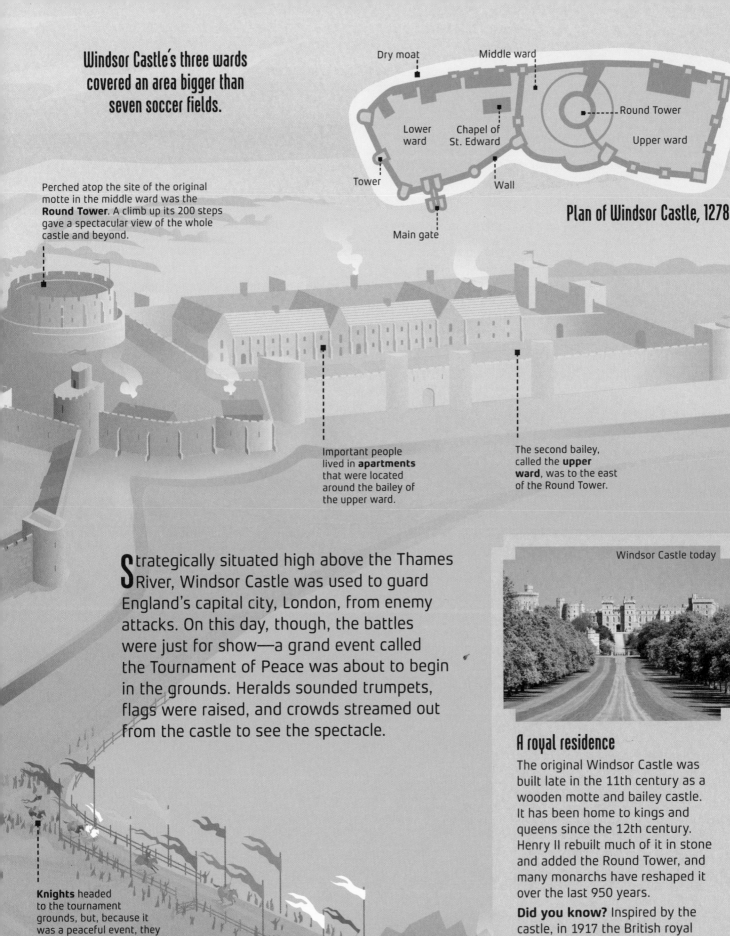

Windsor Castle's three wards covered an area bigger than seven soccer fields.

Dry moat

Middle ward

Round Tower

Lower ward

Chapel of St. Edward

Upper ward

Tower

Wall

Main gate

Plan of Windsor Castle, 1278

Perched atop the site of the original motte in the middle ward was the **Round Tower**. A climb up its 200 steps gave a spectacular view of the whole castle and beyond.

Important people lived in **apartments** that were located around the bailey of the upper ward.

The second bailey, called the **upper ward**, was to the east of the Round Tower.

trategically situated high above the Thames River, Windsor Castle was used to guard England's capital city, London, from enemy attacks. On this day, though, the battles were just for show—a grand event called the Tournament of Peace was about to begin in the grounds. Heralds sounded trumpets, flags were raised, and crowds streamed out from the castle to see the spectacle.

Windsor Castle today

A royal residence

The original Windsor Castle was built late in the 11th century as a wooden motte and bailey castle. It has been home to kings and queens since the 12th century. Henry II rebuilt much of it in stone and added the Round Tower, and many monarchs have reshaped it over the last 950 years.

Did you know? Inspired by the castle, in 1917 the British royal family changed their last name to Windsor.

Knights headed to the tournament grounds, but, because it was a peaceful event, they carried fake weapons. Swords were made of whalebone and painted silver, shields were wooden, and armor was leather.

Inside
Windsor Castle

Queen Elizabeth II of the United Kingdom regularly spends weekends at Windsor Castle. It is the largest occupied castle in the world, hosting banquets, receptions, and meetings with visiting leaders and guests from other countries. Many staff members are needed to keep the castle running, including horologists, who look after the clocks, and fender smiths, who tend to the fireplaces.

The Queen's Guard

In their famous red tunics and tall bearskin hats, the Queen's Guard protects the royal family. They stand in sentry boxes and must try and stay as still as possible while on duty.

St. George's Chapel

St. George's Chapel is much larger than the 13th-century Chapel of St. Edward that it replaced. It was redeveloped in the 15th and 16th centuries and filled with stained-glass windows. In 2018, Prince Harry and Meghan Markle were married at St. George's.

Garter throne room

This was Queen Victoria's throne room, and a throne can still be found here for use by Queen Elizabeth. Today, the room is used to welcome new members to the Order of the Garter—a group of senior knights and ladies.

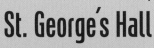

Grand reception room

This room is filled with luxurious items, and it is no wonder that it was once Windsor Castle's main ballroom. Huge chandeliers illuminate the French tapestries on the walls, and in the window stands a large green urn made from the mineral malachite, given to Queen Victoria by Czar Nicholas I of Russia.

St. George's Hall

This is where grand banquets are held. More than 150 guests can sit down to dinner in the long hall. In 1992, a fire destroyed many rooms in the castle, including St. George's Hall, but it has since been repaired.

Beaumaris Castle

Wales, April 1318

In addition to walls almost 16 ft (5 m) thick, six **towers** protected the inner walls of the castle.

Once King Edward I had moved the Welsh residents out of the area, he built a new **town** for English settlers just outside the castle walls.

More than 300 **arrow slits** in the castle walls gave archers a clear shot at any enemy.

Beaumaris Castle would become famous as one of the greatest castles never finished. On the island of Anglesey, just off mainland Wales, King Edward I of England created this stronghold as part of his conquest of Wales. He even moved the nearby town of Llanfaes so he could build Beaumaris. However, the king became distracted by war elsewhere and, although some work continued after his death, the castle was never completed.

Beaumaris Castle today

Unfinished wonder

Edward I built Beaumaris in northern Wales in the late 13th century to stop a Welsh rebellion. Because of a war with Scotland, however, Edward never finished the castle. It was used in the 17th century during the English Civil War, but it later fell into disrepair.

Did you know? Beaumaris was part of the "iron ring" of castles that Edward I built in Wales.

The first line of defense against attackers was a watery **moat**, surrounding the castle's outer walls.

Beaumaris was a **concentric castle**, which means that it was built in rings. Attackers had to cross a moat and break through an outer wall to get to the gatehouse and towers in the middle.

Beaumaris means "fair marsh" in Norman French, referring to the land the castle was built on.

A **dock** ensured that Beaumaris could receive supplies by sea, even if it was under siege.

Plan of Beaumaris Castle, 1318

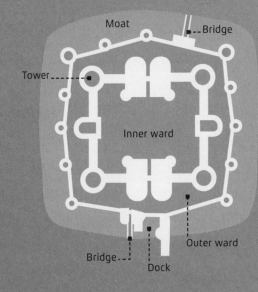

Moat
Bridge
Tower
Inner ward
Outer ward
Bridge
Dock

Ships could sail right up to the dock of this coastal fortress to bring building materials in.

Bodiam Castle

England, June 1391

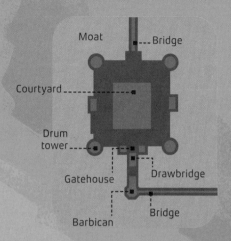

Moat ---- Bridge

Courtyard------

Drum tower----

Gatehouse

Drawbridge

Barbican

Bridge

Sir Edward Dallyngrigge was one of the loyal knights of King Edward III of England. He earned fame and fortune battling the French in 1367, then returned home to marry. Later, when trouble with the French stirred again, he decided to protect his lands by building Bodiam Castle. Unlike some castles, Bodiam didn't change over time. It was built all at once, and was almost perfectly symmetrical. The castle's towers looked even more imposing when reflected in the shallow moat surrounding them.

The main entrance was a three-story **gatehouse** on the castle's northern side. Murder holes and three portcullises kept the castle residents safe.

The **barbican** on an island in front of the gatehouse helped stop any attackers from making their way into the castle. - - -

To cross the moat, visitors had to walk or ride over an L-shaped **bridge**. Anyone trying to storm Bodiam would have to cross over three drawbridges and a barbican while dodging arrows before they could even get to the gatehouse.

The **moat** surrounding the castle also served as a sewer. The toilets in the castle drained straight into its waters. - - - - -

Ponds near the castle filled with huge fish fed the hungry castle residents.

Square stronghold

Bodiam was constructed in southeast England in 1385. Sir Edward received the land Bodiam was built on when he married his wife. In the 17th century, the castle became a ruin and was never repaired.

Did you know? The moat tricked enemies into thinking the castle was taller than it actually was because of its reflective surface.

Bodiam Castle today

Round **drum towers** stood at the castle corners. Unlike other castles, Bodiam had no central keep. The rooms for living, working, and storage were within the castle walls.

A deep **well** underneath the southwest tower was filled by an underground stream.

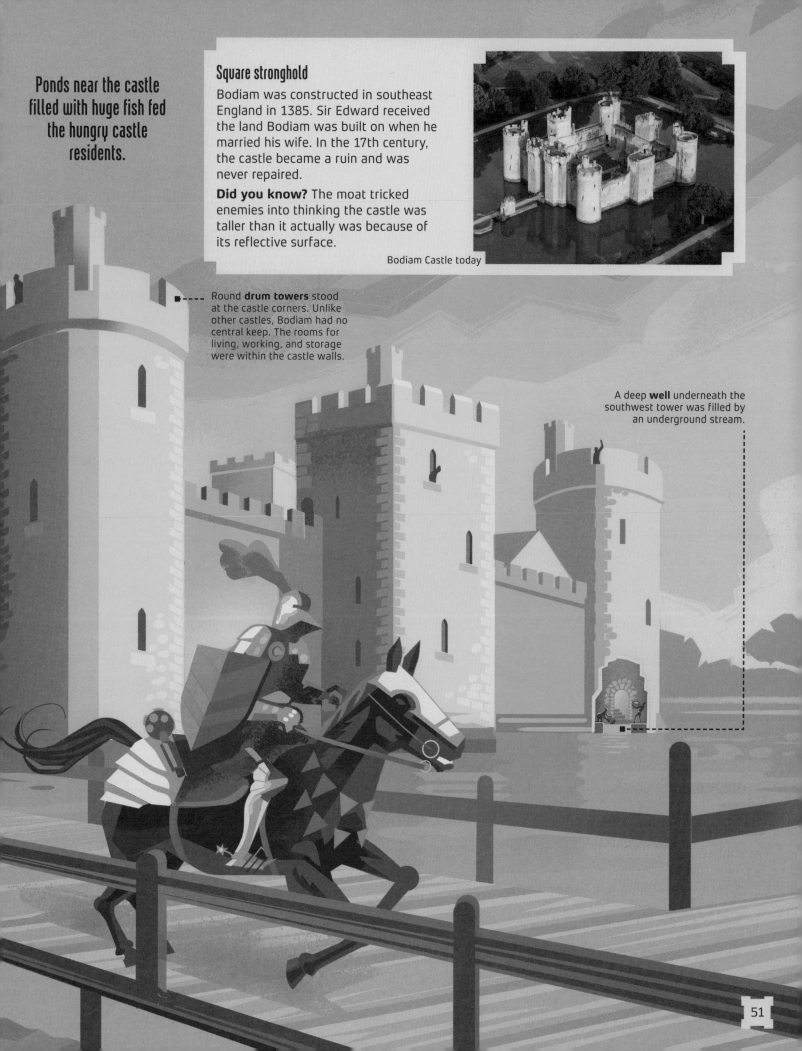

Medieval tournament

Knights sharpened their skills by challenging each other in contests called tournaments. Like sporting events today, tournaments drew huge crowds of cheering fans. Hundreds of knights and their horses took part, in both team events and in individual challenges. Sometimes they fought for prize money, but the respect from winning was its own reward.

Jousting

In this event, a knight and his opponent charged at each other on horseback and tried to knock the other to the ground with a long pole, called a lance. A tournament might last several days, with jousting contests on each day leading to an overall winner.

The **horses** for jousting were trained for speed and flexibility.

A long wooden **lance** was solid enough to strike but also blunt, to prevent injury.

Melee

In this group event, teams of knights fought each other. Each group formed a line and tried to break through the opposition's ranks, armed with clubs, swords, poles, or spears. In another version, every knight fought for himself against the others.

The tournament ground

Tournaments were usually held near the host's castle. An area called a tiltyard was built for jousting contests, with wooden benches for the spectators. Tents made of cloth were set up for each of the competing knights to stay in and store their equipment.

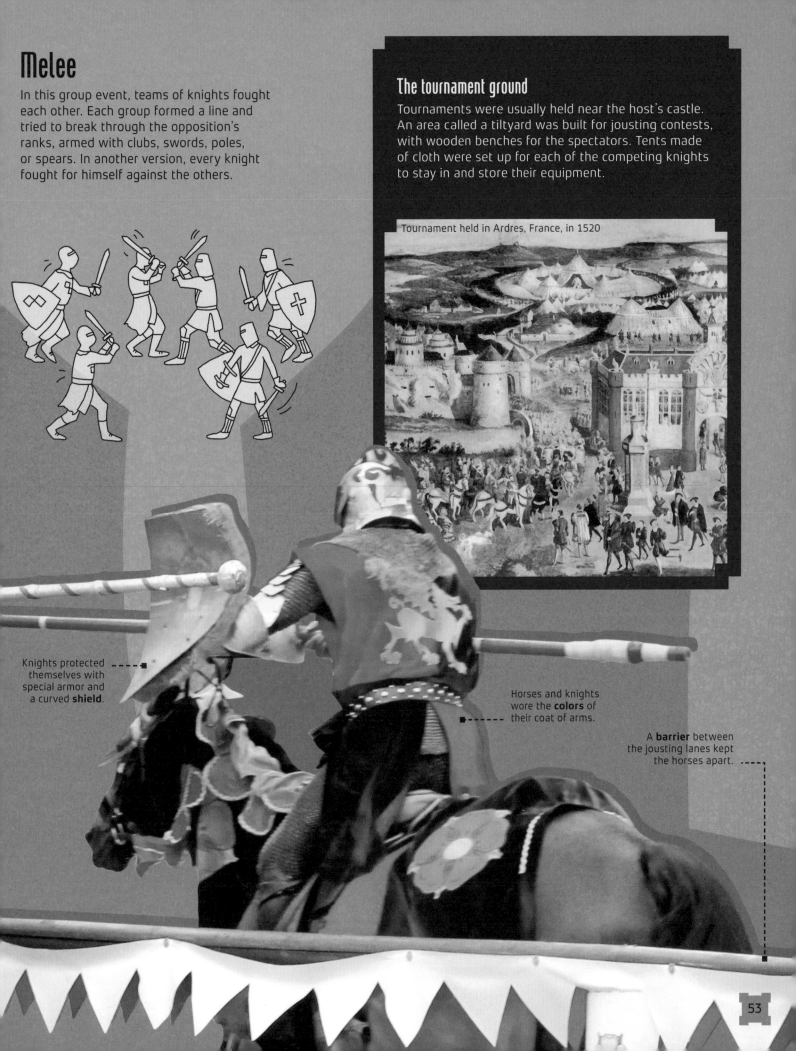

Tournament held in Ardres, France, in 1520

Knights protected themselves with special armor and a curved **shield**.

Horses and knights wore the **colors** of their coat of arms.

A **barrier** between the jousting lanes kept the horses apart.

Bran Castle

Romania, February 1459

The guards watched from the tall towers of Bran Castle as the land's most fearsome ruler approached. It was the notorious warlord Vlad the Impaler, with his rampaging army of soldiers. This time, the castle would be spared— he was on his way to attack the nearby city of Braşov. Still, Vlad attacked the village below the castle, to remind everyone who was in charge.

Vlad the Impaler ruled an area of Romania called Wallachia. He got the name the Impaler from his nasty habit of spearing enemies on spikes.

The castle was built on top of a **cliff**, 200 ft (61 m) tall.

The location of the castle on the edge of **Bran Gorge** made it easier to defend.

Plan of Bran Castle, 1459

Keep

Inner ward

Tower

Vlad's nickname was Dracula, meaning "son of the dragon."

The castle **roofs** were covered in red tiles.

A **secret passage** linked the third and first floors. It provided an escape route if the castle was attacked.

Bran Castle today

Mountain stronghold

Bran Castle was strategically built in the 14th century in a mountain pass between two regions of Romania: Wallachia and Transylvania. In the 20th century, the castle became a summer residence for the Romanian royal family.

Did you know? Bran Castle is sometimes linked to the castle in the book *Dracula* by Bram Stoker—but the castle in the story is fictional (as is the vampire).

The railroad passed through the defensive walls of the castle to reach the keep.

The **keep** contained the lavish Golden Hall and royal apartments.

Around a thousand people worked in the **inner ward**. There were dozens of shops, from bakeries to blacksmiths, and a cistern for water, so the people in the castle could look after themselves.

Hohensalzburg Fortress today

Hilltop castle

Sitting high above the city of Salzburg, Hohensalzburg was originally built in the 11th century by Archbishop Gebhard von Helfenstein. At the end of the 15th century, walls, fortifications, and the railroad were built, which made the castle look much as it does today.

Did you know? From the 16th century, residents in the castle were woken up by the "Salzburg Bull," a pipe organ with more than 200 pipes.

How do you get supplies uphill to a castle? Via a private railroad. The **Reisszug** was built sometime around 1500. Animals or people pulled ropes to bring the wooden car up to the castle.

Hohensalzburg Fortress

Austria, November 1524

Hohensalzburg Fortress towered over the city of Salzburg. In the 15th century, Archbishop Leonhard von Keutschach grew worried about attacks and decided to turn the original fortress into one of the biggest in central Europe. One unusual feature was the railroad built to bring goods up the steep hill to the castle. Leonhard's successor, Archbishop Matthäus Lang, was the only ruler of Hohensalzburg to have to test its defenses when a group of peasants, angry at the archbishops, decided to attack it.

Rings of huge, whitewashed **walls** surrounded the castle, providing layers of defense.

The fortress was built on a rocky hill called **Festungsberg**, with the Salzach River below. The hill was about 1,778 ft (542 m) tall.

Plan of Hohensalzburg Fortress, 1524

Keep

Inner ward

Bastion

Railroad entrance

57

The Reisszug tunnel was blocked up, so the peasants couldn't enter the castle.

Many miners were part of the peasant army. They attempted to dig a **tunnel** under the castle walls to get in, but they didn't succeed.

The peasants were led by **Michael Gaismair**. He wanted a more equal society.

The Peasants' Revolt

Hohensalzburg Fortress, June 1525

The peasants managed to damage the castle badly, alarming the residents inside. A fighting force of some 10,000 of Archbishop Matthäus' **soldiers** assembled to stop the revolt.

Many of the peasants in the German-speaking areas of Europe were fed up. The nobles who ruled them were increasing taxes and demanding extra work. One group near Salzburg, which included miners, farmers, and ordinary people, marched on the city in 1525. They launched a three-month attack on the castle, where Archbishop Matthäus was hiding out in luxurious surroundings.

The **peasant army** had little experience of fighting, but they were determined to be heard. They used what weapons they could find, from clubs to pitchforks.

Failed rebellion

The peasants started a two-year war that raged around central Europe. However, well trained armies wiped out the inexperienced rebels. The peasants in Salzburg agreed a truce with Matthäus, but ultimately nothing changed, and Hohensalzburg remained a castle that was never captured.

Chillon Castle

Switzerland, July 1530

The fabulously wealthy Savoy family lived in this compact castle, positioned between the edge of Lake Geneva and the soaring Swiss Alps. For centuries, anyone foolish enough to oppose the Dukes of Savoy could be sent to its grisly dungeon, as the Swiss monk François Bonivard found out when he challenged the authority of Duke Charles III. He spent six long years locked up in Chillon, before the Bernese captured the castle and freed him in 1536.

From the top of the **donjon**, or main tower, guards could not only look across the lake, but also down on the courtyards below.

The castle's main **defenses** were stone walls with arrow slits and watchtowers. Most of them faced the mountains because an attack from the side that faced the lake was unlikely.

One of the first buildings to be constructed was the **Chapel of St. George**. The Dukes of Savoy worshiped in this beautifully painted room.

Plan of Chillon Castle, 1530

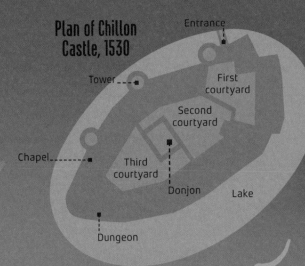

Entrance

Tower

First courtyard

Second courtyard

Chapel

Third courtyard

Donjon

Lake

Dungeon

Chillon completely covered the tiny island it was built on.

Chillon's **location** was very important. Many merchants crossed Lake Geneva and the Alps, carrying goods to trade between Italy and the rest of Europe.

Chillon Castle today

Lakeside lodge

Built in the 12th century by the Savoy family, Chillon Castle protected the mountain trade route to Italy and ships crossing Lake Geneva. It also acted as a post for charging taxes. It was captured by the Bernese in the 16th century and then the Vaudois in the 18th century.

Did you know? English poet Lord Byron visited Chillon and carved his own name into one of the dungeon pillars.

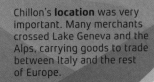

The **dungeon** walls and floors were made of cold, hard rock. The windows were so high that it was almost impossible for François—or any prisoner—to escape.

Lake Geneva is a crescent-shaped lake 224 sq miles (580 sq km) in size. Chillon Castle was built at the eastern point of the lake.

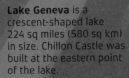

Inside
Chillon Castle

With its fascinating history, grand halls, and windows offering spectacular views of Lake Geneva, it is not surprising that Chillon Castle is the most visited historic building in Switzerland. In the 19th century, parts of it were repaired and restored, but as the castle has never been destroyed in battle, much of what visitors see today has remained the same for centuries.

Bernese chamber

Heating, running water, and its own toilet made this bedchamber very comfortable. A large wooden four-poster bed completed it. In the 17th century, paintings of plants and animals were added.

Chapel

The Dukes of Savoy worshiped here, but later this chapel was used to store goods like grain and gunpowder. It returned to being a chapel in the 19th century. The 14th-century paintings on the walls show people from the Bible.

Aula Magna

The dukes held their feasts and grand receptions here—the largest hall in the castle. No doubt, their guests were impressed by the marble columns, carved wooden ceiling, striped walls, and massive fireplace.

Domus Clericorum

The castle was run from here, the Clerk's Room. Once on two floors, the upper part was destroyed, but the lower room was restored with replicas of the original zigzag wall pattern.

Dungeon

From the 13th century, this cold, dark room in the depths of the castle was where prisoners were kept. Before then, it was used to store weapons and supplies. Some of the castle's rock foundations jut out of the floor.

Down in the dungeon

Often found in the deepest, darkest depths of the castle, the dungeon was the place where prisoners were held captive, and sometimes tortured. A dungeon wasn't always underground, though. Medieval prisoners were sometimes kept in the towering keep, which was tricky to escape from and easy to guard.

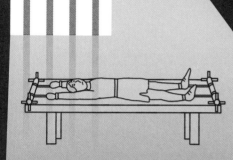

The rack

An unlucky victim of this torture device was secured flat on a board and tied in place. On some racks, there were rollers that could turn to pull the ties tighter and tighter, stretching the prisoner and causing great pain.

Oubliette

Being sent to the oubliette, or "forgotten room," was an awful punishment. Beneath a trap door, the oubliette was a room so small that once a prisoner was lowered inside, he or she could not sit, kneel, or even turn around.

Scold's bridle

A person would think twice about gossiping after being made to wear a scold's bridle. This metal frame was placed around the head and had a metal bit for the mouth to stop the wearer from talking. This punishment was almost always reserved for women.

Manacles and chains

Heavy iron bands, called manacles, locked around the wrists or ankles and attached to chains kept a prisoner from moving far. Adding a weighted ball made escape almost impossible.

Branding

Making a permanent mark on someone's skin with a red-hot instrument was used for torture and punishment. A branding iron was used to make someone give information or to mark a runaway or criminal.

Scavenger's daughter

This hideous device was a hinged iron hoop that held the prisoner's body in a painful position. The scavenger's daughter was usually saved for people who committed treason against the king or queen.

Public punishment

While many terrible tortures took place in the dungeon, others happened in public. Crowds were encouraged to humiliate criminals by jeering, shouting insults, and throwing objects.

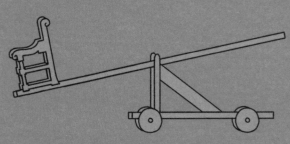

Moat ducking stool

This beam with a chair on one end was placed near the edge of a moat. The victim was strapped to the chair and dunked into the water.

Pillory

The pillory had holes that held a person's head and arms between wooden boards. People threw rocks, rotten vegetables, or worse at the captive.

Gallows

The ultimate punishment was execution. A wooden structure called the gallows was used for hanging. A rope was tied around the prisoner's neck and a trap door was opened under them. As they fell, the rope tightened... and death came soon after.

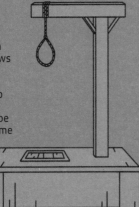

Southsea Castle

England, July 1545

King Henry VIII of England had long worried about enemies crossing the Channel. To prepare, he built a series of forts along the coast, including Southsea Castle, which protected the wealthy city of Portsmouth. Henry was actually inside the castle in 1545 when the French attempted to invade. He sent his fleet to meet the enemy ships, and they managed to repel the French forces, but the English flagship, *Mary Rose*, was sunk.

The **Mary Rose** was Henry's prize ship. It was the first royal English ship to carry cannons on board.

There were rectangular **gun platforms** on both the east and west sides of the castle.

Southsea Castle today

Seaside security

Southsea Castle was built in 1544, with Henry VIII taking a personal interest in the design. It was inhabited and repaired over many years, whenever England needed to guard the coast. It was also used as a prison.

Did you know? In 1828, a lighthouse was added to the castle to help guide ships sailing to Portsmouth.

Plan of Southsea Castle, 1545

Rear bastion

East gun platform

Keep

West gun platform

Forward bastion

Southsea Castle was built quickly, in just six months, because the king feared an attack from France.

The ships weren't in range of Southsea's cannons, but **King Henry** watched from the keep.

Pointed **bastions**—instead of the traditional round ones—made it easier to fire lots of guns at once.

A **curtain wall** surrounded the castle. Gun openings allowed troops to fire on attackers.

Plan of Predjama Castle, 1570

Cave

A **lookout** hole in the cliff connected to the castle via a tunnel.

Upper hall

Tower

Prince's room

Toilet

Bridge

A small room on the third floor housed a **toilet**.

The name Predjama was given to the castle by the noble family who owned it. It means "castle in front of the cave."

The rugged **hills** around the castle are part of the Dinaric Alps. Water has dissolved the rock in this area to create sinkholes and underground caves.

Predjama Castle today

Castle in a cave

Predjama was built in the early 13th century in western Slovenia when the area was part of Italy. According to legend, a knight named Erazem Lueger was besieged in the castle in the 15th century and was killed by a cannonball while he was sitting on the toilet!

Did you know? Predjama is the world's largest cave castle!

The castle was built in a spectacular **cave**, 9 miles (14 km) long.

A **drawbridge** could be pulled up to stop enemies from entering the cave castle.

Predjama Castle

Slovenia, November 1570

This handy cave led down the mountain, making it perfect for a stealthy **escape**. Horses were kept in one of the caverns.

Secret passages, a colony of bats, and a legendary death in the john. Welcome to Predjama Castle. This incredible fortress was built at the entrance to a vast cave. The first castle on the site was destroyed by a siege, and an immense earthquake ruined its replacement. It was rebuilt in 1570 so its sturdy square towers filled the cave mouth.

Heidelberg Castle

Germany, September 1618

The residents of Heidelberg Castle raised their glasses together in front of one of the world's largest wine barrels. Their ruler, Friedrich V of the Palatinate, joined them, but he was in no mood to celebrate. The conflict between the Catholic Holy Roman Emperor, Ferdinand II, and the Protestant parts of the country had begun a conflict that would become the Thirty Years' War. The Protestants wanted Friedrich to lead them, but it would mean leaving the safety and beauty of his castle.

The eight-sided **Bell Tower** was originally a gun turret, but it was built higher over many generations.

Gunpowder was stored in the **Powder Tower**.

Friedrich set out to charm his English wife, Elizabeth, with the **Palatine Garden**. Created in terraces around the castle, it featured an orange grove, fish ponds, and chirping mechanical birds.

Plan of Heidelberg Castle, 1618

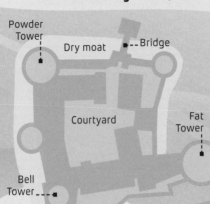

Powder Tower
Dry moat
Bridge
Courtyard
Fat Tower
Bell Tower

The Friedrich Building was lined with rows of statues of the rulers of the Palatinate.

Heidelberg Castle today

Palatinate palace

Founded in the 13th century, Heidelberg Castle was the residence of the Counts of the Palatinate. Much of it was destroyed in a war with France in the 17th century. In the 19th century, it was partly restored.

Did you know? According to myth, a witch tried to bite through the metal ring on the gate in order to become the owner of the palace. However, she only succeeded in breaking her teeth!

To create a regal residence fit for an English princess, Friedrich built the **English Building**, a palace within the castle.

The **Friedrich Building** had apartments for the family and servants' quarters in the attic. A grand terrace at the front provided sweeping views of the town below.

As another surprise gift to his wife, Friedrich created the **Artillery Garden**, a private space within the castle walls.

In around 1533, Ludwig V built the **Fat Tower**. Its walls were 23 ft (7 m) thick.

In 1591, a massive **barrel** that could hold 34,000 gallons (130,000 liters) of wine was built at the castle. Building these huge barrels was a bit of a competition in the area.

What's inside a castle?

Bedroom

The lord or lady and their family typically slept in the warmest part of the castle. The family might have a suite of rooms for privacy, including a living room and a dressing room.

Kitchen

Castle cooks needed large kitchens to prepare the food and store the equipment for everything from a simple breakfast to a three-day feast. Some castles had more than one kitchen to be able to feed all the residents.

Dungeon

Many castles were not built with underground dungeons, so prisoners were kept in other secure parts of the castle. However, as holding captives became more common around the 12th century, basement dungeons started to be built.

A castle was used in times of war, but it was also a home. You may not have a great hall, a moat, or a well in your house, but all the typical rooms are also found in most castles. They may have been fancier and larger, but they shared the same functions as in houses today. Castles often had hundreds of occupants so needed lots of space.

Great hall

The great hall was the main dining area for the castle. The hall often had a large fireplace and sometimes served as a sleeping area for guests and members of the castle staff.

Chapel

Religion was very important in medieval life, and most castles had a chapel that was used every day for prayer and also for important ceremonies, such as weddings.

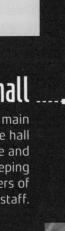

Well

A well was essential for everyday use, and especially important if the castle fell under a siege, when no supplies could get in. A well dug deep underground ensured a constant flow of water.

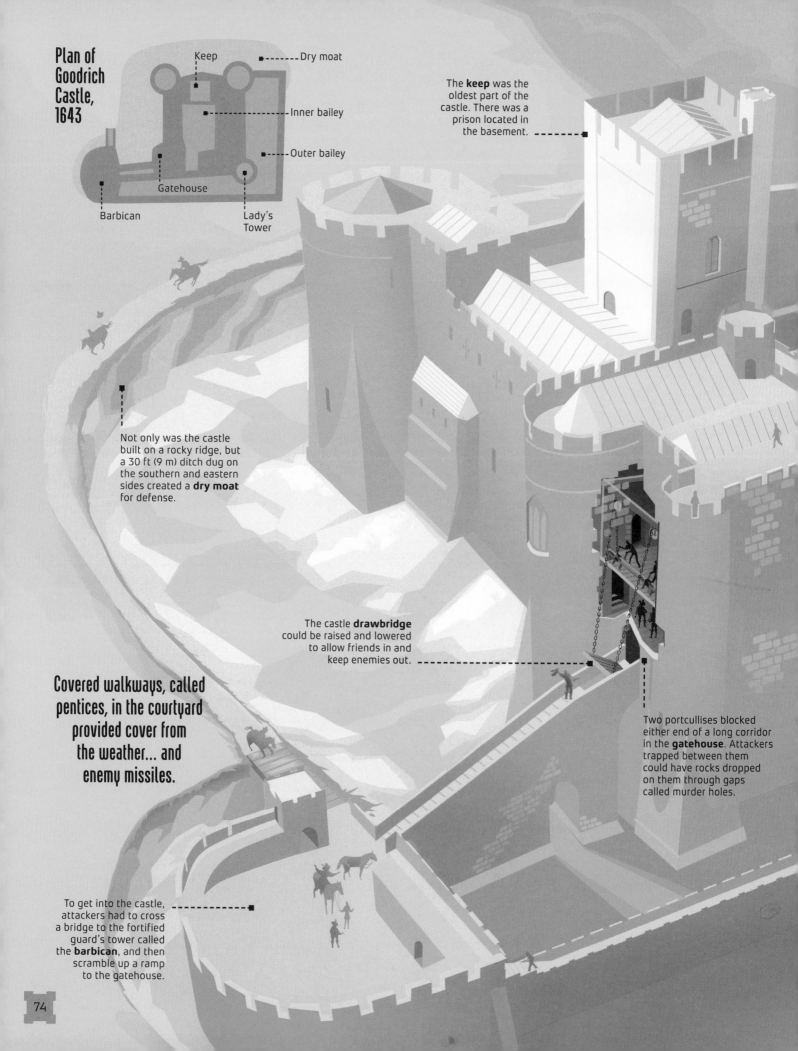

Plan of Goodrich Castle, 1643

Keep

Dry moat

Inner bailey

Outer bailey

Barbican

Gatehouse

Lady's Tower

The **keep** was the oldest part of the castle. There was a prison located in the basement.

Not only was the castle built on a rocky ridge, but a 30 ft (9 m) ditch dug on the southern and eastern sides created a **dry moat** for defense.

The castle **drawbridge** could be raised and lowered to allow friends in and keep enemies out.

Covered walkways, called pentices, in the courtyard provided cover from the weather... and enemy missiles.

Two portcullises blocked either end of a long corridor in the **gatehouse**. Attackers trapped between them could have rocks dropped on them through gaps called murder holes.

To get into the castle, attackers had to cross a bridge to the fortified guard's tower called the **barbican**, and then scramble up a ramp to the gatehouse.

Goodrich Castle

England, December 1643

The small castle **courtyard**, built around 1300, was surrounded by the chapel, great hall, and living quarters for officers and servants. About 200 people lived in the castle at busy times.

The **Lady's Tower** was the residence of the mistress of the castle. Large windows let warm sunshine pour into the rooms.

A **postern gate** could be used for escape if the main entrance was being attacked.

Overlooking the pretty green countryside and a winding river, who could imagine a more peaceful setting than Goodrich Castle? Yet this fortress was caught up in the English Civil War. Good friends had become bitter enemies. King Charles I and Parliament were locked in a power struggle for the right to rule, and both sides wanted control. First, Parliamentarian forces set up camp in the castle, then Charles's supporters, the Royalists, took it over... but the Parliamentarians wanted it back.

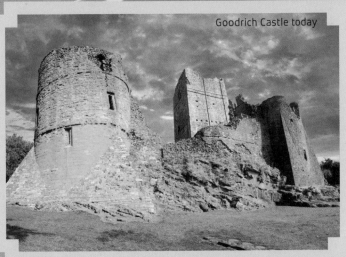
Goodrich Castle today

The castle of Godric

Godric of Mappestone built the first Goodrich Castle from wood in the 12th century on land that bordered England and Wales. It was later rebuilt and expanded in stone. However, during the English Civil War in the 17th century, the castle was reduced to ruins.

Did you know? According to legend, two ghosts of people who died during the Civil War haunt the castle.

Cannon attack

Goodrich Castle, July 1646

In the middle of summer, the Parliamentarians decided to lay siege to Goodrich and capture it once and for all. There were around 170 Royalist soldiers in the castle. First, the Parliamentarians cut off the defenders from their main water supply. Next, they dug tunnels to weaken the castle walls and, finally, they unleashed Roaring Meg, a gigantic cannon. Kaboom! The Lady's Tower was soon in ruins.

Royalist soldiers were known as **Cavaliers**, meaning "horsemen." They supported King Charles I.

Roaring Meg could unleash a 200 lb (85 kg) shell filled with explosive gunpowder. Not even the strongest castle walls could withstand that kind of onslaught.

Parliamentarian soldiers were known as **Roundheads** because they wor their hair short.

The Parliamentarians thought the **Lady's Tower** was a weak spot and concentrated their attacks on it. They destroyed a large part of the tower using Roaring Meg.

Siege success

The Parliamentarian leader, Colonel John Birch, sent a letter to the Royalist commander Sir Henry Lingen asking him to surrender. At first, Henry refused, so the siege continued. Eventually, the Royalists gave in, and the castle was "slighted," or partly demolished, so it couldn't be used again.

The Parliamentarian leader ordered his troops to dig **mines** under the castle walls to try to make them fall down.

The Royalists dug a **countermine** under the Parliamentarian mine to try to destroy it, but it collapsed when the Lady's Tower was attacked.

Becoming a knight

Many a young boy dreamed of becoming a knight. A brave soldier might be awarded a knighthood for excellence in battle, but the other path to knighthood was a little more complicated. Through years of training and studying, a boy could become a knight's apprentice and then, with a tap of the sword, become a knight himself.

Page

A boy started knight training when he was seven. He lived with a lord or knight, doing chores and delivering messages. He also learned reading and writing, hunting, and fighting.

Each squire was given his own **sword**. He promised to use it with respect and honor. - - - - - -

Squire

At 14, a page became a squire. He was given specific jobs in the lord's home, such as cleaning armor or serving at banquets. His training intensified, and he learned to fight while wearing armor.

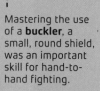

Mastering the use of a **buckler**, a small, round shield, was an important skill for hand-to-hand fighting.

Code of chivalry

Studying manners and social skills was as important to trainee knights as learning how to fight. Following the code of chivalry—a way to behave with courage, kindness, and courtesy—marked a true knight.

Only a wealthy family could afford a suit of **armor**, so knights were often sons of nobles.

Wearing the family coat of arms on a **shield** helped others identify a knight.

Squire in training

In addition to looking after a lord or knight and learning his manners, a squire's training involved plenty of combat practice. It was tough work, sometimes made harder with heavier weapons so that a real fight would seem easier.

Hand-to-hand combat, such as **wrestling,** helped to develop a squire's physical strength.

Building flexibility through **acrobatic** training helped a young squire learn to be more agile.

A spearlike **javelin** could be thrown at enemies. It took a lot of practice to aim it correctly.

Squires used a heavy wooden pole, called a **quarterstaff**, to strike their opponents, even in practice.

Knight

At 21, a squire could become a knight. During the knighting ceremony, he was dubbed, or tapped on the shoulder with a sword, confirming him as a knight.

Knights needed excellent **horseback-riding** skills.

Elmina Castle

Ghana, May 1670

The castle was a safe harbor for slave ships. Thick **walls** and cannons aimed toward the sea defended the castle against attacks from rival traders.

Slaves were kept in the **dungeons** for up to three months. There was not even room to lie down, and diseases spread quickly.

Slave ships arrived at the castle to trade their goods, which included cloth, guns, metals, beads, and other valuables, for a cargo of slaves. In the Americas, the ships' captains traded the slaves for sugar, tobacco, rubber, and cotton.

Canoes were used to transport slaves from the shore to the slave ships.

Elmina Castle today

Slave port

Elmina was built by the Portuguese King João II in 1486 as a trading post for ivory and gold. By the 17th century, however, the castle was used mainly to imprison slaves. In 1637, the Dutch captured the castle, and it was used as part of the slave trade until 1814.

Did you know? In the early 16th century, nearly a tenth of the world's gold came from the region around Elmina.

The **governor's rooms** were luxurious and a striking contrast to the horrible conditions in the dungeons below.

Imagine a medieval castle, and you might not picture palm trees, sandy beaches, and ocean waves crashing under blue skies. Elmina Castle was famous for its seaside setting and its beauty. Yet its thick white walls hid something shocking: the castle was a hub for the slave trade. Thousands of Africans were captured and held prisoner at Elmina, before being sent on ships to the Americas to be sold. Countless people suffered in the terrible conditions of the castle's dungeons.

The materials used to build Elmina were shipped to Ghana from Europe.

Plan of Elmina Castle, 1670

Keep

Slave market

Dungeons

Dungeon

Slaves were imprisoned in one of the castle dungeons. These long stone rooms were very uncomfortable, with little light, space, or fresh air. There were no toilets or beds and up to 1,000 prisoners could be crammed inside together.

Door of no return

Just before prisoners were taken to the ships, they passed through a passage and then a doorway to the outside. These were only big enough for one person to go through at a time.

Condemned room

Prisoners who displeased the guards could end up in the condemned room. This was a tiny space where slaves were left to die without any food or water. A skull and crossbones was positioned above its black door.

Slave market

Surrounded by the castle's tall white walls, the slave market was the main building in the courtyard. It was previously a church, but was converted so slave traders could buy prisoners at auctions.

Inside Elmina Castle

For centuries, this former trade route rest stop was a key center of the slave trade. Thousands of slaves were sent in ships from Elmina to the Americas. Today, Elmina Castle hosts many visitors who hope to better understand its history. People can explore both the dungeons, where the prisoners were kept, and the upper floors, where the slave traders lived.

Cannons

Located right on the beach, Elmina Castle was vulnerable to attacks from the sea. The Europeans who ran the castle, afraid of the threat of rival traders, positioned cannons on the walls, aimed at the ocean.

In 1327, King Edward II died suspiciously at Berkeley Castle while being imprisoned there. Many historians think he was murdered.

The circular **shell keep** was added around the base of the original motte, to strengthen its defenses. Uneven "trip steps" inside slowed down any enemy invaders.

In 1327, King Edward II was kept in a small **cell** next to the keep after his wife, Queen Isabella, and an enemy nobleman invaded England and captured him.

A **curtain wall** was added to the bailey after the stone keep was constructed.

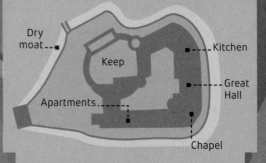

Plan of Berkeley Castle, 1728

Dry moat
Keep
Kitchen
Great Hall
Apartments
Chapel

The **Chapel of St. Mary** had parts of the Bible written on its ceiling in Norman French.

Berkeley Castle

England, June 1728

Berkeley Castle was originally built to defend England against attacks from the Welsh, but it was later used to imprison King Edward II. With tall stone walls and stained glass windows, this spectacular castle was home to the Berkeley family for hundreds of years, and they often entertained. One summer's evening, guests enjoyed an amusing performance from Dicky Pearce, a court jester. However, during his show he fell—or was pushed—from a balcony in the Great Hall and died.

The most important room in the castle was the **Great Hall**. This was where the lords of Berkeley entertained their guests.

A **jester** entertained people with jokes, magic tricks, and acrobatics.

Berkeley Castle today

Family fortress

Built in western England by William FitzOsbern, a relative of King William I, Berkeley was originally an 11th-century motte and bailey castle. It was rebuilt in stone over many years. Except for a brief gap, the Berkeley family has lived here for more than 800 years.

Did you know? A hole made in the walls of the castle during the English Civil War of the 17th century was forbidden to be repaired—and it never has been!

Organistrum

Two players operated this stringed instrument. One person turned the crank that made the sound, while the other pressed down on keys to change the notes. The players sat down with the organistrum on their knees.

Rebec

The pear-shaped rebec looked a little like a modern violin. Players held the instruments on their arms while running a bow across the strings and pressing the strings with their fingers to change the notes.

Tabor

Pipers who wanted to add a beat while they played banged a drumstick on the tabor. This small drum had an animal skin stretched across its round frame that made a sound when hit.

Music

Whether part of the entertainment at a banquet or a bright fanfare to announce the start of a special event, music often rang through the castle halls. There was singing and chanting as well as an array of musical instruments to play. Musicians called minstrels sang tales of brave knights and fierce battles.

Herald's trumpet

Blowing into a trumpet made a loud sound that got everyone's attention. Heralds used them to announce the start of a banquet or special event, such as a wedding. Unlike a modern trumpet, it played just one note.

Pipe

A simple tube-shaped instrument, a pipe was made of wood, metal, or a hollow reed. Players covered a combination of the holes as they blew air through the tube to create musical notes.

Bagpipes

The bagpipes were played by inflating the leather bag and then squeezing it under the arm to push the air out of the pipes. Some of the pipes made a fixed sound, while one pipe had holes so a melody could be played.

Song and dance

Dancing was a popular activity for all classes. A noble family in a castle might hold a ball where guests danced together. Everyone would know the set steps to the dances.

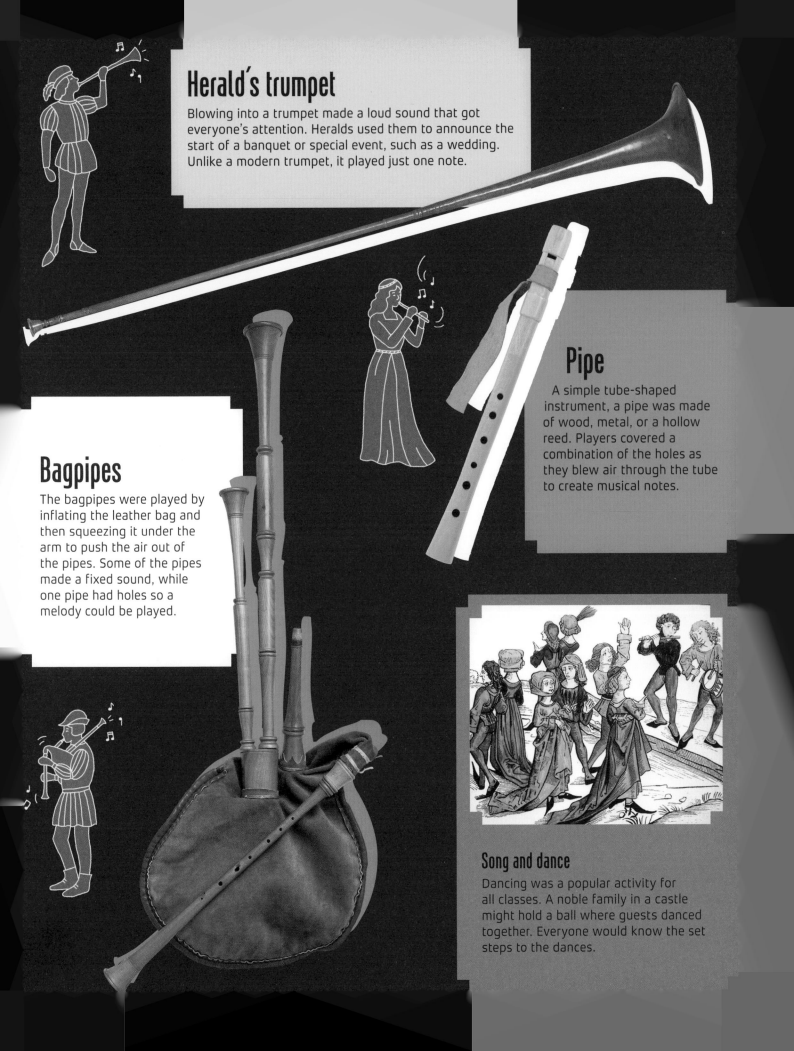

Scaligero Castle today

Safe harbor

The Della Scala family built Scaligero in northern Italy in the 13th century to protect themselves during a conflict with the Dukes of Bavaria. The castle was captured by Napoleon's French forces in the early 19th century before falling into disuse.

Did you know? There are 146 steps up to the castle battlements.

There has been a fortress where Scaligero Castle stands since ancient Roman times.

The keep and battlements had **crenellations** with "swallow-tail" edges, which the Della Scala family, who built the castle, particularly favored.

The tiny town of **Sirmione** was outside the castle walls.

Three **towers**, each about 52 ft (16 m) high, protected the central keep.

Scaligero Castle

Italy, September 1804

A floating fortress? It seemed impossible, but Scaligero Castle was built in the waters of Lake Garda. When the Napoleonic Wars, led by Emperor Napoleon I of France, spread across Europe, the castle became a weapons store and barracks for the French forces. They kept watch for enemies from the tall ramparts, while boats delivered supplies to the walled port attached to the castle.

The castle's **walls** surrounded the lake's edge to make a protected harbor for ships and boats.

Walkways inside the harbor meant defenders could patrol the walls.

The castle was surrounded on all sides by water. The only way in or out was via two **drawbridges**, which connected the castle to the mainland.

Plan of Scaligero Castle, 1804

Lake

Drawbridge

Keep

Harbor

Drawbridge

Alhambra Palace

Spain, August 1808

In 1533, Charles V, the powerful Emperor of Spain, destroyed some of the earlier buildings and started to build the **Charles V Palace**. However, it was never finished.

The Alhambra was originally painted white, but the paint has fallen off over time, revealing the red walls.

Three palaces, known as the Nasrid Palaces, surrounded a large **pool** 112 ft (34 m) long. This pool would have been a great luxury, as water was scarce in this part of the country.

Spectacular **arches** inside the palace were decorated with carvings and writing, handcrafted with only a few simple tools.

The **Comares Tower** contained the Hall of the Ambassadors, where the king sat on his throne to meet with official guests.

Alhambra Palace today

The red castle

The Alhambra was built in the 9th century near the southern coast of Spain. Sultan Mohammed I, founder of the Nasrid Kingdom, created the first palace on the site in the 13th century and many Nasrid rulers added to it. In the 15th century, King Ferdinand II and Queen Isabella I of Spain set up their court in the fortress, but it was eventually abandoned.

Did you know? Local legends tell of a rich treasure buried underground and protected by a genie.

A grand palace complex rising above the Spanish city of Granada, the Alhambra had a strategic view of the entire city below. For centuries, the fortress had been ruled by the Nasrid sultans, who built grand palaces and gardens, then it was taken over by the Spanish, and later abandoned in the 18th century. When Emperor Napoleon's French forces arrived in 1808, there was no one to defend the castle and they destroyed it further.

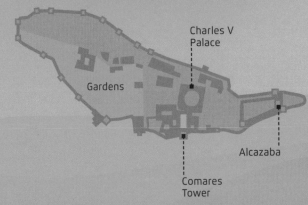

Plan of Alhambra Palace, 1808

Charles V Palace

Gardens

Alcazaba

Comares Tower

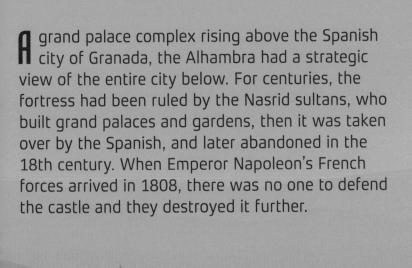

The Nasrid sultan Mohammed I added a tall watchtower to the **Alcazaba**, one of the oldest parts of the fortress.

The outer **walls** of the palace complex were built from damp soil pressed into frames. Alhambra means "the red castle" in Arabic, possibly because of the reddish color of the soil used to make it.

Inside
Alhambra Palace

Alhambra Palace attracts millions of visitors each year. They come to admire its majestic buildings, courtyards, and gardens, but especially the incredible skill in the decorations covering the walls and structures of the palace. In particular, the Nasrid Palaces found in the west of the Alhambra are filled with multicolored tiles and Arabic inscriptions. Much of the decoration is carved out of stucco, a type of plaster.

Arches

Every space in the Alhambra is painted, tiled, or carved, including the intricately engraved arches. Many of the arches are for display only, and were not built to support the palace's structure. The designs include winding plants and calligraphy—words written in beautiful letters.

Tiles

Colorful ceramic tiles decorate many of the palace walls in intricate repeating patterns. The pigments used to create each color were made from natural materials, such as iron, copper, and tin.

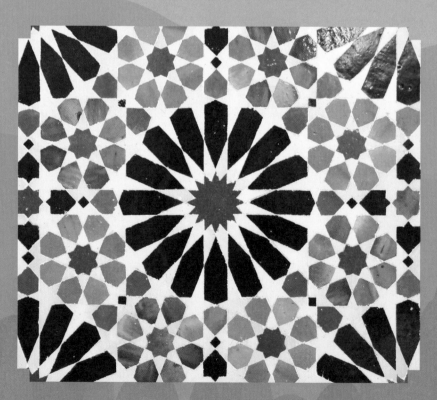

Patio de los Leones

The Court of the Lions is found within the Nasrid Palaces. It contains a fountain with a dozen marble lions that shoot jets of water from their mouths. A covered walkway with 124 columns provided shelter from the baking sun.

Patio de los Arrayanes

This courtyard is also known as the Court of the Myrtles because of the green myrtle hedges now growing around its rectangular pond. The water comes from two trickling fountains, one at either end.

Armor

Battles were brutal in medieval times. Arrows rained down from the sky, axes and swords slashed and struck, and hammers and clubs delivered a wallop. Knights protected themselves with a suit of armor. This was often custom-made and had many different parts to protect every part of the body.

Tilting armor

Tilting armor was worn during jousting competitions at tournaments and had holes where it could be attached to regular armor. Knights needed more protection on their left side, since this side was nearer to their opponent.

Suit of armor

Helmet

Pauldron

Breastplate

Vambrace

Gauntlet

Plackart

Fauld

Cuisse

Poleyn

Greave

Sabaton

Leather armor could be made of small linked pieces to make it easier to move in.

Leather armor

An alternative to costly metal armor was specially treated leather. The leather was boiled in water, then molded into shape, becoming harder and tougher. Leather armor was also more flexible than metal.

Chain mail

Early knights depended on flexible armor made of metal rings linked together. This armor, called chain mail, was fairly easy to move in but also provided all-important protection from swords and arrows.

Wealthy knights had their armor engraved with fancy designs.

Leather straps helped fasten the plates together and added some flexibility.

Plate armor

In the 14th century, weapons improved and chain mail no longer gave enough protection. Knights wore suits of solid metal plates that could weigh 55 lb (25 kg).

Equipment

A suit of plate armor included various accessories that protected different parts of the body. Making the suit in sections helped the knight bend at the joints to get the full range of movement he needed.

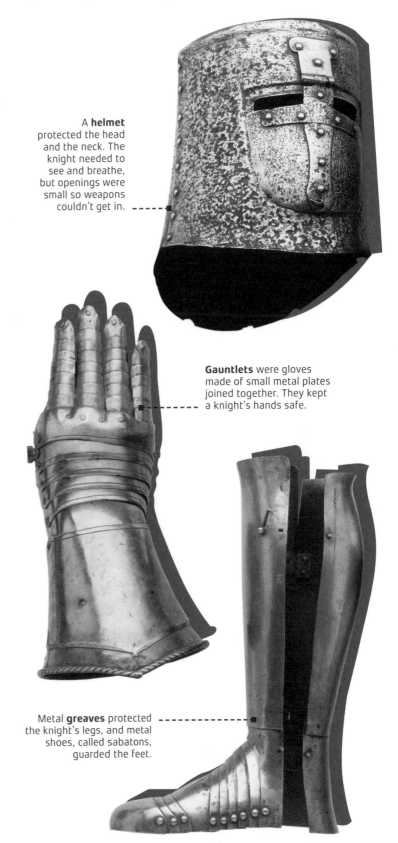

A **helmet** protected the head and the neck. The knight needed to see and breathe, but openings were small so weapons couldn't get in.

Gauntlets were gloves made of small metal plates joined together. They kept a knight's hands safe.

Metal **greaves** protected the knight's legs, and metal shoes, called sabatons, guarded the feet.

Mehrangarh means "fort of the sun."
The royal family was believed
to be descended from the Hindu
sun god, Surya.

The **Palace of Flowers** was a grand room decorated with gold, mirrors, and paintings of Hindu gods. The maharaja invited important guests here to enjoy entertainment, such as dancing.

The fort was built on a 400-ft (122-m) tall **cliff** above the city of Marwar.

Cannons on the ramparts could blast away an approaching enemy.

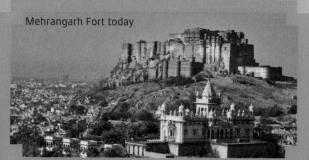
Mehrangarh Fort today

Fort in the sky

Mehrangarh was built in the 15th century by Maharaja Rao Jodha, above his new capital city, named Marwar—now Jodhpur. During a war with the rival city of Bikaner in the early 19th century, cannonball scars were left on its walls.

Did you know? According to legend, a man was buried under the fort's foundations. This was meant to guarantee good fortune.

Mehrangarh Fort

India, August 1813

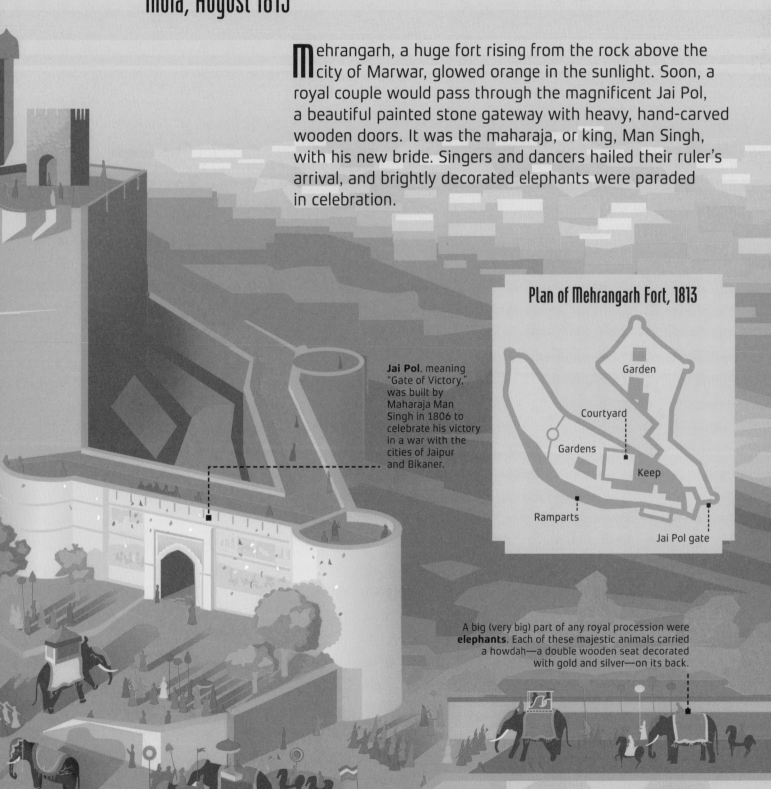

Mehrangarh, a huge fort rising from the rock above the city of Marwar, glowed orange in the sunlight. Soon, a royal couple would pass through the magnificent Jai Pol, a beautiful painted stone gateway with heavy, hand-carved wooden doors. It was the maharaja, or king, Man Singh, with his new bride. Singers and dancers hailed their ruler's arrival, and brightly decorated elephants were paraded in celebration.

Jai Pol, meaning "Gate of Victory," was built by Maharaja Man Singh in 1806 to celebrate his victory in a war with the cities of Jaipur and Bikaner.

Plan of Mehrangarh Fort, 1813

Garden

Courtyard

Gardens

Keep

Ramparts

Jai Pol gate

A big (very big) part of any royal procession were **elephants**. Each of these majestic animals carried a howdah—a double wooden seat decorated with gold and silver—on its back.

Pearl Palace

There were several palaces within the fort complex. Maharaja Saw Raja Sur Singh created the huge Moti Mahal, or Pearl Palace, in the 16th century. The walls glow a pearly white in lamp light because of the seashells crushed into the plaster, and the windows are filled with colorful panes of glass.

Palace of Mirrors

Almost every surface of the Sheesh Mahal, or Palace of Mirrors, is covered in glass and mirrors. This palace, built in the 18th century, was part of the private rooms of Maharaja Ajit Singh. The original ceiling is now displayed on the floor.

Palace of Flowers

The Phool Mahal, or Palace of Flowers, is a highly decorated palace built by Maharaja Abhay Singh in the 18th century. Guests were received in its single room, designed to impress with golden walls and paintings.

Inside
Mehrangarh Fort

Many maharajas have lived in Mehrangarh Fort since its creation. It is still owned by members of the same clan as Maharaja Man Singh. Today, Mehrangarh is open to visitors and contains a museum filled with a collection of royal objects. Climbing the slope to reach the fort is an impressive journey. The exterior is majestic, but the insides, restored to show what life was like living at Mehrangarh, are just as amazing.

Maharaja's bed chamber

In the Takhat Vilas, bedroom of Maharaja Takhat Singh, almost every surface is painted, from the wooden ceiling to the floor. Constructed in the 19th century, there are countless pictures on the walls. In the 1930s, large, shiny Christmas ornaments were hung from the ceiling.

Murals

Mehrangarh Fort is filled with murals—pictures painted directly onto walls. These colorful images show everything from Hindu gods and goddesses to portraits of the maharajas.

Base colors

Gules

Purpure

Vert

Sable

Azure

Metals

Or

Argent

Furs

Ermine

Vair

Colors

The simplest badge of identity was a color. In heraldry, colors were known as tinctures, and all had a special name. Some were metallic and others were animal fur designs.

Lions

Gules (red)

Heraldry

Friend or foe? If a knight encountered another knight on the battlefield, how could he tell who was inside the suit of armor? In medieval times, royals, nobles, and knights displayed symbols on their banners, shields, and clothes to identify themselves. The practice became known as heraldry. Each mix of colors and signs was called a coat of arms, and the different parts had different meanings.

Richard "the Lionheart"

Three lions on a red background has long been a symbol of England. King Richard I, also known as Richard "the Lionheart," created it in 1198. The lions are still used by the English national soccer team.

Ordinaries

To create more variety between coats of arms, shapes called ordinaries were added. These divided the coat of arms into sections. Ordinaries also have their own names.

Charges

Charges were pictures of objects, animals, or even mythical beasts. Each charge was usually simple enough to be spotted at a distance, and to be easily copied onto shields and banners.

Dragon

Sun

Lion

Eagle

Unicorn

Fleur-de-lys

Fess

Pale

Chief

Chevron

Cross

Saltire

Bend

Pall

Pile

Japanese kamon

In Japan, noble families created their own special symbols, called kamon. These were used just like a coat of arms. They were usually circular in shape, and often displayed symbols of plants, flowers, and animals. Sometimes kamon were included in the design of a castle, too.

On a clear day, the view from the castle stretched for 60 miles (100 km).

The Catholic **St. Michael's Chapel** was built at the south end of the U-shaped castle.

The Protestant **Christ's Chapel** sat at the north end of the castle.

There was no worse fate than being trapped in a **zwinger**, a narrow gap between an inner wall and an outer wall that made attackers easy prey. The zwinger at Hohenzollern zigzagged around the castle.

Hohenzollern Castle

Germany, October 1867

There had been a castle at Hohenzollern since the 11th century, but not one like this. King Frederick William IV of Prussia, a descendant of the Hohenzollern family, had visited the site in 1819 and found only the crumbling remains of a medieval fortress. He decided to rebuild it with a grand entrance and ornate turrets rising above the clouds. Unfortunately, the king died in 1861, but six years later Hohenzollern was ready to receive guests once again.

Royal guests could enter through the **Eagle Gate**—if the drawbridge was lowered for them.

Plan of Hohenzollern Castle, 1867

Bastion

Count's Hall

Christ's Chapel

Watchtower

St. Michael's Chapel

Eagle Gate

Outer wall

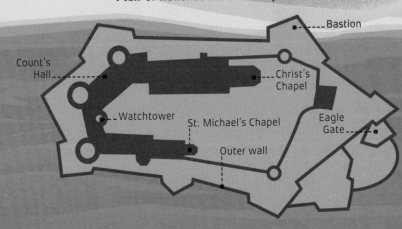

Hohenzollern Castle today

Hohenzollern the third

The Hohenzollern family built the original castle in southwest Germany in the 11th century. It was replaced by a stronger second version in the 15th century, but that fell into disrepair. Finally, the castle as it looks today was finished in 1867.

Did you know? A ghost, known as the White Lady, is said to roam the halls of Hohenzollern Castle.

Kumamoto Castle

Japan, February 1877

The akazu-no-mon gate to the castle was never opened, to keep out bad spirits.

The lord of the castle lived and greeted his official guests in the **Honmaru Goten** palace. Gold leaf decorations and paintings adorned the impressive main hall.

The **tenshukaku**, or castle keep, was almost 100 ft (30 m) tall and had six stories.

The **Tsuboi River** running along the east side of the castle complex helped protect it from attack.

The **Satsuma army** was approaching. The warriors were planning to besiege Kumamoto to drive out the government's Imperial Army.

Kumamoto Castle was built to be the ultimate stronghold. The fortified complex contained a keep, palace, 49 turrets, 29 gates, sturdy stone walls, moats, arrow slits, and plenty of holes for dropping missiles on anyone trying to attack. However, that didn't put off some very determined soldiers. The samurai warriors of the Satsuma area of Japan were angry with the government and had gathered an army to march on Japan's capital, Tokyo. First, though, they had to pass through Kumamoto Castle.

Plan of Kumamoto Castle, 1877

Moat

Turret

Keep

Honmaru Goten palace

Tsuboi River

Bridge

The **musha-gaeshi** were tall, curving walls found at the bottom of important buildings. The walls got steeper as they rose, making them hard for attackers to climb.

Kumamoto's **turrets** gave castle defenders a good spot to keep watch and a platform for launching attacks. Extra weapons were stashed in them, too.

A ring of stone **walls** surrounded the castle grounds.

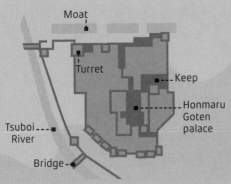
Kumamoto Castle today

Complex castle

Built on the site of a smaller castle from the 15th century, Kumamoto Castle was created in the 16th century by Kato Kiyomasa, a powerful daimyo. It was partly destroyed during the Satsuma Rebellion in the 19th century. The castle was repaired but has been repeatedly damaged by earthquakes, including one in 2016.

Did you know? The tatami mats that covered the castle floors were filled with vegetable stalks so they could be eaten during a siege.

The Satsuma Rebellion
Kumamoto Castle, February 1877

A fire had broken out a few days before the attack, destroying a large food store, and the defenders covered the castle gates with **canvas** to hide the damage.

The fighting forces of the government's **Imperial Army** knew they had to fend off the attack to stop the area around Kumamoto from falling to the rebels.

Kumamoto Castle was about to face its toughest test. The Satsuma army, led by legendary samurai warrior Saigo Takamori, had surrounded its walls. There were around 4,400 defenders from the Imperial Army inside the castle led by Major General Tani Tateki. For two months they fought, but Kumamoto did not fall. The arrival of thousands of extra Imperial Army troops sent the Satsuma warriors running. The two sides met again and clashed in a series of battles, but, by September 1877, the Satsuma Rebellion had failed.

The **Satsuma army** had twice as many soldiers as the Imperial Army, many of them trained samurai warriors.

Before the siege began, the Imperial Army had raced to stock up on **food supplies** inside the castle.

Both sides fought with guns and swords. The Satsuma warriors carried **long swords** that were 3 ft (1 m) long.

Weapons

A knight or a samurai relied on his weapons. It took a great deal of training and skill to be able to wield a sword, ax, or mace while riding a horse or wearing a heavy suit of leather or metal.

Swords were blades wielded with one or two hands.

A heavy **mace** had a club on one end that was sometimes spiked.

A **battle-ax** could be thrown, swung, or used to hook an opponent's shield and lift it away.

Knight

Skilled, brave, educated, and loyal, knights were soldiers who earned respect through their service to the king or queen. Protected with heavy suits of armor, they swung and slashed their deadly weapons with skill, whether on horseback or in one-on-one combat.

Knight's armor

Overlapping plates of metal made up the **croupiere** to protect the horse's back legs.

A knight's horse had a **chanfron** to protect its head.

A **peytral** covered the horse's chest.

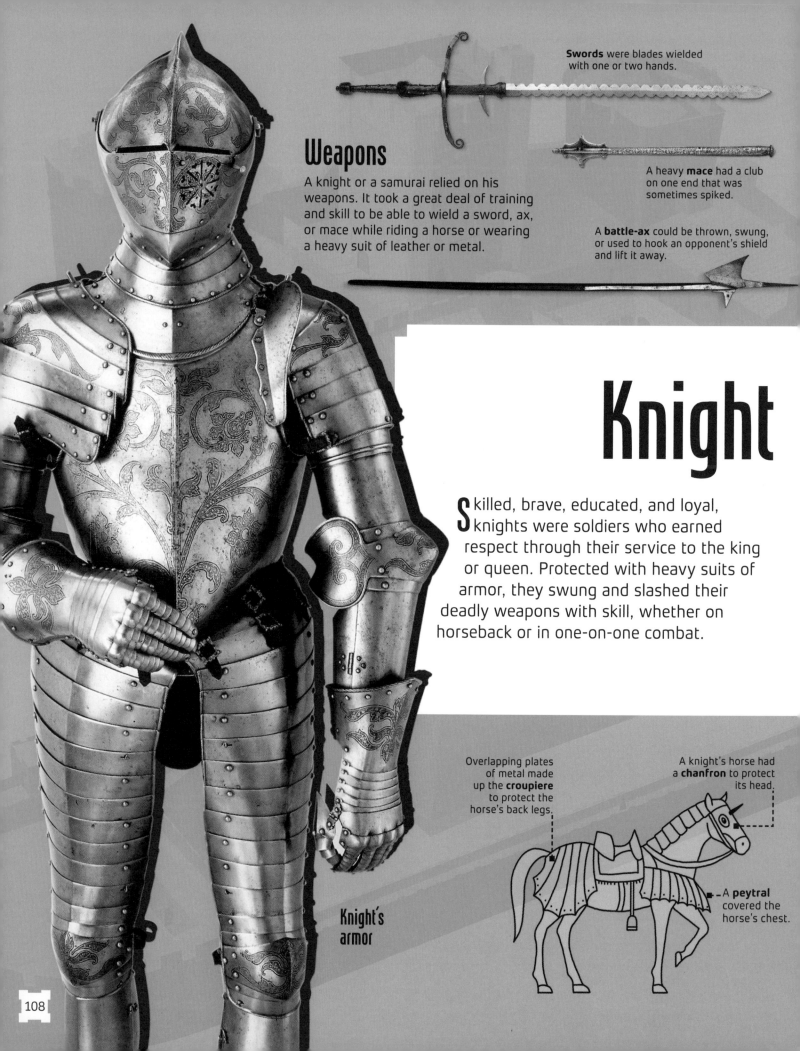

A samurai often carried two types of sword, including a long sword called a **katana**.

A pole with a blade on top, the **naginata** could be used at a distance.

The **uchine** was a deadly throwing arrow that could also be used at close range.

A **wakizashi** sword had a shorter blade than a katana, and was used in close-quarter combat.

Samurai's armor

vs. samurai

The same qualities valued in a knight were also looked for in a Japanese samurai warrior. A samurai used weapons with deadly precision, but also relied on quick thinking to outwit his opponents. Like a knight, a samurai practiced self-discipline and respect for others.

A samurai's horse sometimes had a mask shaped like a **dragon's head**.

Horses

Perhaps the most important asset for a knight or samurai was his horse. Samurai were the only Japanese warriors allowed to ride horses into battle, and both knights and samurai spent hours training on horseback.

Tiles of **leather** created body armor.

The **palas** contained the servant's rooms on the lower floors and the king's rooms on the upper floors. Ludwig even asked for a fake cave to be built inside!

The elaborate **throne room** was found on the top two floors of the palas—the main castle building. It was never finished and it never contained a throne.

Neuschwanstein means "New Swan Stone." This name was inspired by the Swan Knight, a character from an opera that Ludwig enjoyed.

One of the paintings on the front of the palas showed the legendary **St. George** killing a dragon.

The stone **courtyard** was split across two levels. The open terraces allowed visitors to gaze out over lakes and lush forests.

Neuschwanstein Castle today

Fairy-tale castle

Neuschwanstein was built in southern Germany in the 19th century for the personal enjoyment of King Ludwig II. It was never completed, but that didn't stop it from becoming a popular tourist attraction.

Did you know? Ludwig himself spent only a handful of nights in his magical castle before his death.

Neuschwanstein Castle
Germany, April 1884

It was nearly lunchtime, but as flurries of snow sprinkled down on the fairy-tale towers of Neuschwanstein Castle, King Ludwig II of Bavaria was still fast asleep. He had taken to spending all night awake, sometimes in costume, and all day in bed while his dream castle was being built. With very little real power, Ludwig wanted to build a fantasy world around himself. Neuschwanstein was Ludwig's grand project, but he died in 1886 before it was completed.

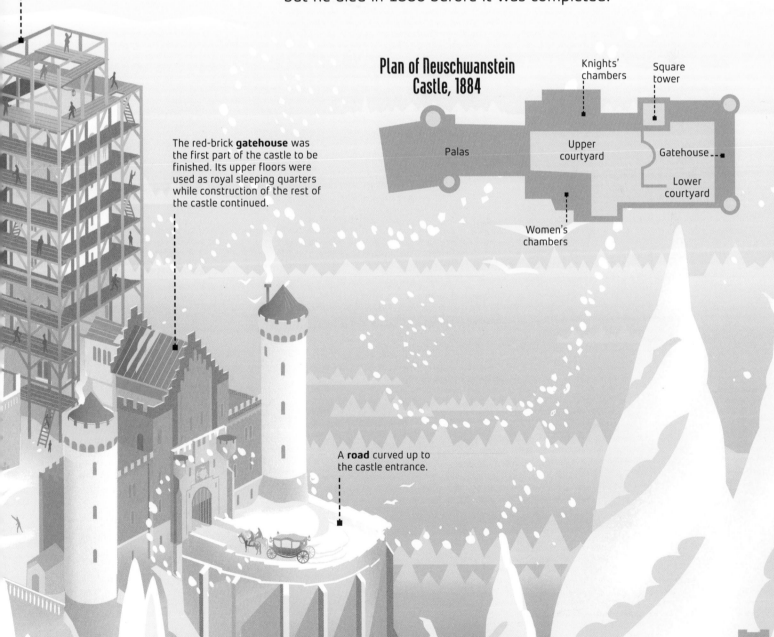

Many people were working hard to finish Ludwig's castle. However, the square tower and the upper courtyard were **not completed** before King Ludwig II died.

The red-brick **gatehouse** was the first part of the castle to be finished. Its upper floors were used as royal sleeping quarters while construction of the rest of the castle continued.

Plan of Neuschwanstein Castle, 1884

Knights' chambers

Square tower

Palas

Upper courtyard

Gatehouse

Lower courtyard

Women's chambers

A **road** curved up to the castle entrance.

Throne room

Ludwig died before he could put a throne in this elaborate hall. The huge room occupies two stories of the palas and contains a chandelier that is 13 ft (4 m) tall. The golden walls are painted with religious figures, plants, and animals.

Singers' Hall

Despite its name, this hall was not used for singing, or any other performances. Instead, King Ludwig built it as a tribute to the legendary knights he admired. It was inspired by rooms in Wartburg Castle.

Kitchen

The well-equipped kitchen had a large oven, heated drawers for keeping plates warm, and even a tank so fish could be cooked and served fresh. Ludwig did not keep regular mealtimes, so the chefs had to be ready to cook at any time.

Inside
Neuschwanstein Castle

King Ludwig saw his castle as a monument to the medieval age. Its walls were covered in paintings of heroic knights, myths, and legends. He wanted Neuschwanstein to be absolutely perfect; however, his death in 1886 meant the castle was left unfinished. Less than two months after Ludwig died, the castle was opened to the public, and today it is a popular tourist attraction.

King's bedroom

The king's ornate bedroom was filled with wooden carvings, from the walls to the bed. Dotted around the room are symbols of swans, one of Ludwig's heraldic signs, including the miniature fountain that filled the sink.

Picture cycles

Throughout the castle are many murals—pictures painted on the walls—inspired by the medieval legends that also inspired Wagner's operas. These include stories of the knights of King Arthur and Norse gods.

Castle of Good Hope

South Africa, March 1901

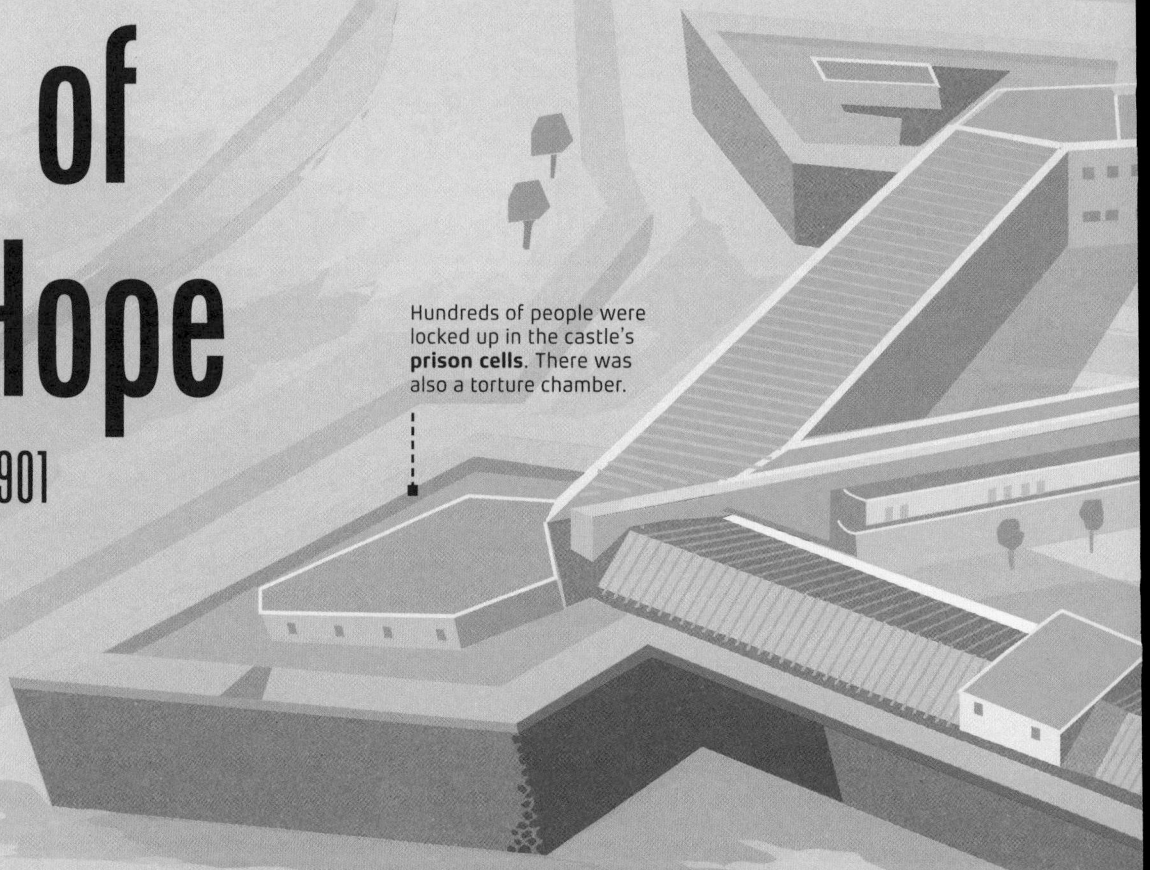

Hundreds of people were locked up in the castle's **prison cells**. There was also a torture chamber.

A star-shaped fortress on the shores of Cape Town, the Castle of Good Hope was built to be tough. A crew of sailors, soldiers, and slaves built the huge structure under the orders of the Dutch East India Company, a large Dutch trading business, to serve as a stopping place between Europe and Asia. The British took over the castle, and during the Second Boer War, which was fought between the British Empire and parts of southern Africa, it was used as a prison.

Plan of the Castle of Good Hope, 1901

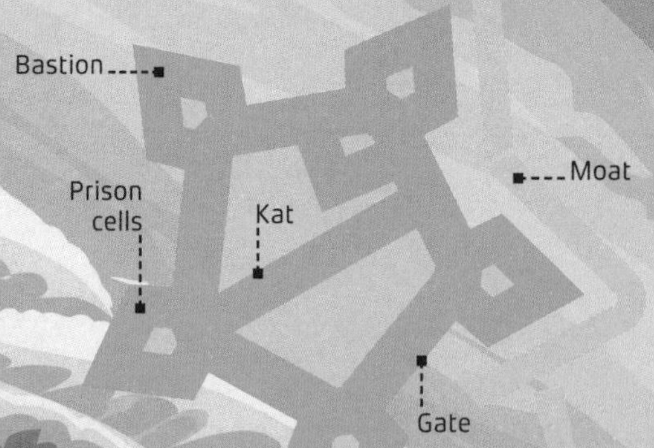

Bastion

Moat

Prison cells

Kat

Gate

The Castle of Good Hope was built from granite, slate, and seashells.

To help slow down attackers, a huge wall called the **Kat** was built across the inner courtyard of the castle. It also contained offices for officials.

The **yellow paint** on the walls was chosen to stop the glare of the blazing sun. The light color reflected heat, keeping the castle cool.

This **entryway** was not part of the original castle, but was added in 1682. A bell tower above it contained a huge 660 lb (300 kg) bell. When it rang, soldiers and residents rushed to the castle for news.

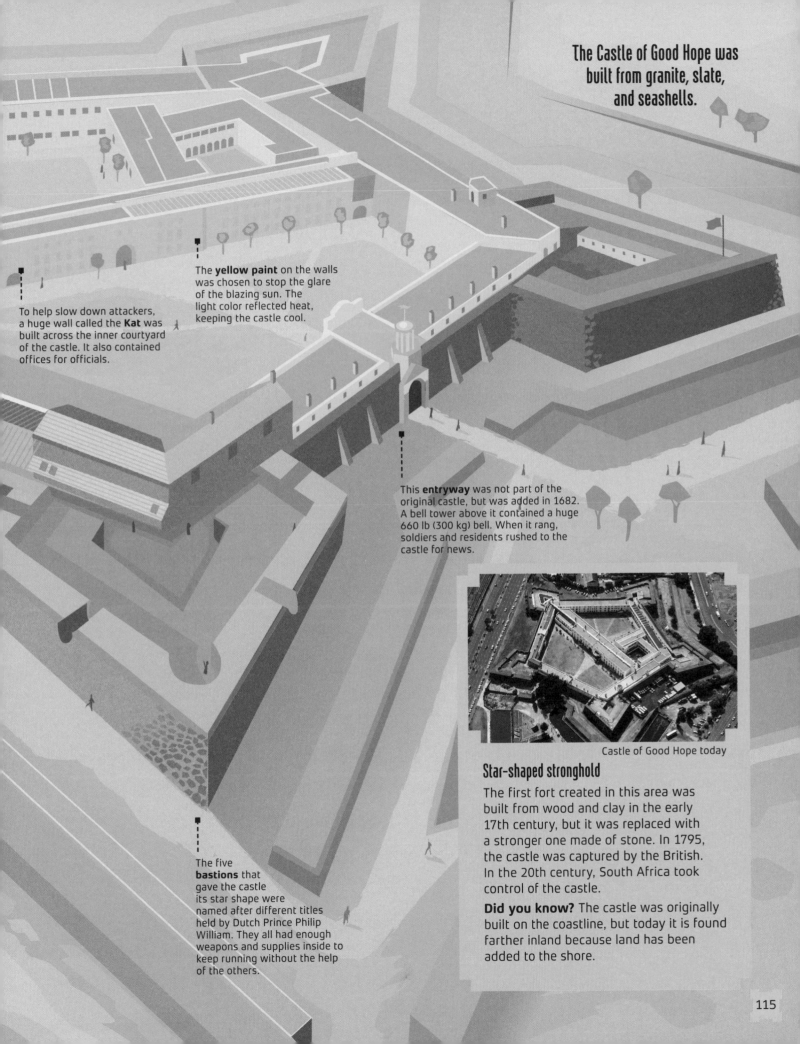

Castle of Good Hope today

Star-shaped stronghold

The first fort created in this area was built from wood and clay in the early 17th century, but it was replaced with a stronger one made of stone. In 1795, the castle was captured by the British. In the 20th century, South Africa took control of the castle.

Did you know? The castle was originally built on the coastline, but today it is found farther inland because land has been added to the shore.

The five **bastions** that gave the castle its star shape were named after different titles held by Dutch Prince Philip William. They all had enough weapons and supplies inside to keep running without the help of the others.

To destroy the evidence of his digging, Fritz threw each spoonful of mortar out through the open bars of his prison **window**.

Digging to freedom

Castle of Good Hope, April 1901

The castle's stone **walls** were incredibly thick—some were even said to be cannon-proof. Deep foundations supported the heavy walls, and to make them even sturdier, some of the walls were built in two layers and filled with clay.

There wasn't much hope for the people imprisoned in this castle. The British owners were fighting the Boers in the Second Boer War, and captured enemies were sent to cells in the castle. Among them was Fritz Joubert Duquesne, a spy for the Boers. Fritz had escaped many prisons, but in 1901 he found himself in the Castle of Good Hope. Did he have a chance of getting out of this castle fortress?

Fritz could not charm or bargain his way out of the castle, but he did have an iron **spoon**. A little at a time, he dug away at the mortar, the mixture holding the bricks of the wall together. He worked night after night to loosen the stones so that he could escape.

Fritz Joubert Duquesne

Fritz had a lifelong dislike of the British, so he joined the fight when local Boer forces waged war against them. He was repeatedly captured, but always managed to escape. After his attempted escape from Good Hope, Fritz was sent to a prison on the island of Bermuda, but again he escaped and later settled in the United States.

Only the best Dutch **bricks** were used to build the castle. The mortar, made from burned seashells and sand, was also of the highest quality. ---------■

Trapped in the tunnel

One night, Fritz had made just enough of a hole in the wall to squeeze himself through. He slithered through the makeshift tunnel, but a heavy stone slipped down and pinned him in place. His escape plans foiled, he was found unconscious the next morning by a prison guard.

Great escapes

Storming a castle to get in was hard, but imagine how difficult it was for a castle captive to get out. Often locked in a dungeon, there were thick stone walls, moats, and guards to overcome. However, some daring and desperate prisoners managed to make an escape.

The chest

Dutch lawyer Hugo Grotius was sent to Loevestein Castle in the Netherlands during a political war. His wife often sent him a huge chest of books to read. One day, Hugo slipped inside the chest—and slipped past the guards.

The keys

Queen Mary I was kept in Lochleven Castle during a fight for the crown of Scotland. A party was arranged and when the castle inhabitants were drunk, a young boy stole the castle keys so Mary could escape.

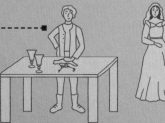

The boy covered the keys with a handkerchief and whisked them away.

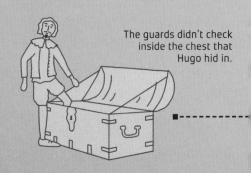

The guards didn't check inside the chest that Hugo hid in.

The secret message

John Gerard was a priest who was held in the Tower of London for his religion. He wrote a message in invisible ink to his friends, who rowed a boat up to the Tower to help Gerard get away.

Gerard climbed down a rope and joined his rescuers in the boat.

The sewer

Notorious knight Erazem Lueger was imprisoned in Ljubljana Castle in Slovenia for murder. Even though the castle was heavily guarded, Erazem managed to escape. Some suggest that he exited through the sewer, or perhaps bribed a guard.

One of the only ways to get out of the castle unseen was the same way waste flowed out—through the sewer.

The prisoners tunneled out of the castle. The hole in the wall is still visible today.

The tunnel

Edinburgh Castle in Scotland was used to hold prisoners captured in the Napoleonic Wars. In 1811, a group of 49 French prisoners chiseled through the stone defenses and then used ropes to climb down the walls. They fled, but were all recaptured.

The glider

During World War II, a team of British prisoners held at Colditz Castle, Germany, worked together to build a glider—a plane without an engine—hoping to sail over the castle walls. They were freed, however, before they finished it.

The glider has been reconstructed today. Originally, prisoners used bedframes, floorboards, and cloth to build the glider.

Himeji Castle

Japan, July 1945

Himeji Castle's hilltop site gave it a towering view over the city below. This beautiful castle was used as a lord's residence and barracks for warriors from the 16th century. During World War II, American bomber planes arrived to attack the city of Himeji, which had an important railroad station. Much of the city was destroyed, but the castle escaped the falling bombs... almost.

Himeji was nicknamed the "white heron castle" because of its white walls and curved roofs.

During the attack, the main part of the castle was covered in **camouflage netting** to help hide it from the air. Its height, hilltop location, and gleaming white walls would have made Himeji easy to spot.

The castle's wooden frames were coated in a thick layer of **white plaster**, made from lime, ash, and seaweed. The plaster helped make the walls fire-resistant.

One **bomb** actually fell through the roof into the top floor of the keep, but, amazingly, it didn't explode.

Plan of Himeji Castle, 1945

Turret

Keep

Outer walls

Moat

Moat

Gate

More than 100 aircraft headed toward Himeji city during the air attack on July 3, 1945, including one of the largest bomber planes of World War II, the **B-29 Superfortress**.

Standing 151 ft (46 m) tall was the huge **keep**. From the outside, it looked as if there were only five floors, but there were actually six floors and a basement hidden by stonework.

Himeji Castle today

The white heron castle

Himeji was built in southwest Japan by Kuroda Shigetaka in the 16th century on the site of an earlier castle. It was expanded in the early 17th century. The castle fell out of use but survived plans to destroy it and multiple earthquakes.

Did you know? During a powerful earthquake in 1995, a bottle of sake (rice wine) placed on an altar in the castle did not spill a drop.

Inside
Himeji Castle

There are many castles in Japan, but Himeji is perhaps the most incredible due to its condition and enormous size. The castle complex is made up of more than 80 buildings, connected by winding pathways and multiple gates that were designed to confuse attackers. Today, visitors can wander the mazelike grounds and—in springtime—marvel at the dazzling cherry trees in blossom.

Roof tiles

Overlapping curved tiles cover the roofs of the towers, walls, and gates. Each vertical row of tiles ends with a specially made disk marked with the kamon, or crest, of the family that built that section of the castle.

Sama

The triangular, square, or circular holes in the castle walls are called sama. Defenders could shoot through the sama, which were positioned at different heights for use when standing or kneeling. The holes narrowed on the inside so arrows and bullets were less likely to get in.

Ishiotoshi

Some walls include projections called ishiotoshi. These have openings in the bottom that are similar to murder holes found in European castles. Defenders could spy on intruders from them, or throw stones and boiling water onto attackers.

Wooden core

Giant trunks of fir and cypress trees support the structure of the keep. The flexible wood helps the castle to sway in an earthquake, instead of crumbling. Himeji is mostly made from wood and white plaster, including the interiors.

Roof guardians

Decorative statues of a half-tiger, half-fish creature called a shachihoko mark the ends and corners of the castle roofs. It was believed that they would protect the building against fires.

Hearst Castle

USA, August 1929

Two **bell towers** decorated with blue and gold tiles were modeled on a Spanish church. There were 18 bells in each tower that were rung by pressing the keys on a keyboard.

The main house on the estate, **Casa Grande**, contained Hearst's own suite as well as many bedrooms and bathrooms, and a library.

In the evenings, guests gathered in the **Assembly Room**. They were required to meet their host for a drink in this elaborate space before enjoying a lavish meal.

The outdoor **Neptune Pool** was the site of many parties. It was decorated with sculptures of the Roman god Neptune and mythical water creatures called nereids.

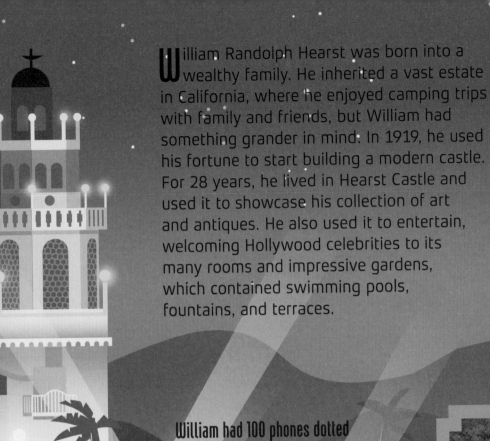

William Randolph Hearst was born into a wealthy family. He inherited a vast estate in California, where he enjoyed camping trips with family and friends, but William had something grander in mind. In 1919, he used his fortune to start building a modern castle. For 28 years, he lived in Hearst Castle and used it to showcase his collection of art and antiques. He also used it to entertain, welcoming Hollywood celebrities to its many rooms and impressive gardens, which contained swimming pools, fountains, and terraces.

Plan of Hearst Castle, 1929

Casa Grande

Casa del Monte

Neptune Pool

Casa del Mar

Casa del Sol

William had 100 phones dotted around the estate so he could keep in touch with people—one was even behind a tree on the horse-riding trail.

Hearst Castle today

Hollywood hangout

Hearst Castle was built on the West Coast of the United States. An invitation there was prized by everyone. Guests included Hollywood stars, such as actors Charlie Chaplin, Greta Garbo, and Cary Grant, as well as leading politicians such as British Prime Minister Winston Churchill. Today, the castle contains a museum.

Did you know? The castle had its own runway so that visitors could arrive by airplane.

A spectacular **fountain** topped with a bronze statue welcomed guests to the Casa del Sol.

Castles collection

From the earliest brick fortresses to beautiful stone citadels and modern recreations, there are countless impressive castles that can still be found around the world. They can't possibly all fit onto the pages of this book, so here's a glimpse at some more of the globe's most glorious castles.

Czocha Castle

This 13th-century Polish castle was built by King Wenceslaus I of Bohemia. A fire destroyed it in the 18th century, but it was restored.

Did you know? It was rebuilt in the 20th century, based on a painting of the castle before the fire.

Arg-e Bam Citadel

Constructed more than 2,000 years ago in Iran, this citadel was built on the Silk Road, a trade route that linked Europe and Asia. In 2003, an earthquake destroyed much of it.

Did you know? Arg-e Bam is the largest adobe, or mud, structure in the world.

Bahla Fort

This giant fortress was built in the 12th century by the Nebhani dynasty in Oman. It is constructed from mud bricks on top of sandstone foundations.

Did you know? Soldiers used to pour boiling date juice onto attackers through the murder holes in the fort.

Hochosterwitz Castle

People have lived atop this Austrian hill since the Bronze Age and there has been a castle here since the 9th century. In the 16th century, the castle was expanded to how it looks today.

Did you know? The winding road leading up to the castle has 14 fortified gates.

Prague Castle

Built in the 9th century in the Czech Republic by Prince Bořivoj of Bohemia, this castle was originally made from wood. It was rebuilt in stone from the 12th century and one tower even had a golden roof added.

Did you know? The castle houses the Czech Crown Jewels.

Kilkenny Castle

Founded in the 12th century in Ireland, this castle was built by Norman nobleman Richard de Clare. It was originally made out of wood, before being rebuilt in stone in the 13th century.

Did you know? For nearly 600 years, the castle was owned by the same family.

Gravensteen

Translated as "The Castle of the Counts," Gravensteen was built by Philip of Alsace, one of the Counts of Flanders. Constructed in Belgium in the 12th century, it replaced an earlier castle.

Did you know? Gravensteen has been used as a prison, a court, and a cotton mill.

Burghausen Castle

Started in the 11th century, this castle in Germany was expanded in the 13th century. Built along a narrow ridge, the castle grounds are divided up into five courtyards.

Did you know? This is the world's longest castle. It stretches for more than 0.6 miles (1 km).

Citadel of Cairo

This gigantic citadel in Egypt was built by the Muslim sultan Saladin as a defense against Christian Crusaders in the 12th century. The Pyramids of Giza can be seen from its windows.

Did you know? The huge citadel contains three large mosques.

Mont-Saint-Michel

This tiny island off the coast of France was originally home to a church built in the 8th century. A town appeared around it, and in the 13th century strong defenses were added.

Did you know? Before a bridge was built, the path to the island was regularly submerged by the tide.

Falak-ol-Aflak Castle

This ancient castle, built in the 3rd century in Iran at the time of the Sasanian Empire, is positioned at the top of a hill. Only eight of its original 12 towers survive today.

Did you know? This castle is known by as many as five different names.

Castel Nuovo

This castle in Italy was built in the 13th century for King Charles I of Anjou, but, due to war, he never lived there.

Did you know? From 1443, King Alfonso V of Aragon rebuilt the castle and added a two-story white marble arch.

Srebrenik Fortress

Constructed in the 14th century in Bosnia and Herzegovina, this medieval castle sits on a tall, rocky hill, accessible only by a bridge, which made it easier to defend.

Did you know? Its outer walls are 5 ft (1.5 m) thick.

Anadoluhisarı

Founded in the 14th century in Turkey by Sultan Bayezid I, this castle sits on the edge of a narrow strip of water called the Bosphorus.

Did you know? A twin castle called Rumelhisarı was built on the other side of the Bosphorus.

Leeds Castle

This English castle sits in the middle of a lake. In 1119, nobleman Robert de Crevecoeur replaced a 9th-century wooden building with the stone castle. It has been used as a prison and a hospital.

Did you know? Today, the castle contains a dog collar museum.

Citadel of Qaitbay

This fortress in Egypt was constucted in the 15th century by Sultan al-Ashraf Qaitbay to defend the coast.

Did you know? The fortress was built on the same spot as the Lighthouse of Alexandria, one of the Seven Wonders of the Ancient World.

Mendoza Castle

This mighty castle was built from strong granite in Spain in the 15th century by Duke Diego Hurtado de Mendoza and his son as a grand fortress to live in.

Did you know? The towers have false machicolations, for decoration rather than defense.

Osaka Castle

This castle was built in Japan in the 16th century by the daimyo Toyotomi Hideyoshi. It was rebuilt in the 17th century following wars, fire, and even being struck by lightning.

Did you know? When it was built, this was the biggest castle in Japan.

Fortaleza Ozama

Originally a watchtower, Fortaleza Ozama was built by the Spanish in the Dominican Republic in the 16th century. It is named after the nearby Ozama River.

Did you know? The fort is partly constructed from blocks of coral from the sea.

Red Fort

The Red Fort was built by Emperor Shah Jahan in the 17th century in India. It contains many ornate buildings and gardens.

Did you know? The fort gets its name from the red sandstone that it is built from.

Lichtenstein Castle

This cliff-top castle in Germany was built by Count Wilhelm von Urach in the 19th century in the style of a medieval castle.

Did you know? It was constructed on top of the foundations of an older 14th-century castle.

Belvedere Castle

This miniature castle in the United States wasn't built to be used for defense. Created in the 19th century, it stands in Central Park in New York City and is used to view the surrounding park.

Did you know? In Italian, Belvedere means "beautiful view."

Aït Benhaddou

Fortified in the 11th century, this village in Morocco has crenellated towers and is surrounded by a high wall. The buildings inside are made of red mud bricks.

Did you know? It has been used as a film location for many movies.

Grand Palace

This huge complex in Thailand was created in the 18th century as the official home of King Rama I. Its defensive walls surround more than 100 buildings.

Did you know? A Buddhist temple in the complex contains a statue of Buddha made from green jade.

Alcázar of Segovia

Found in central Spain, this castle was transformed over time from a Roman fort to a wooden Almoravid castle and, finally, to a stone fortress. Much of it was rebuilt in 1862 following a fire.

Did you know? Several secret passageways connect the castle to the nearby rivers.

Chapultepec Castle

This grand castle in Mexico was built as a home for Viscount Bernardo de Galvez in the 18th century. In the 19th century, Emperor Maximilian I moved his court there.

Did you know? The castle functioned as an observatory for a short time.

Malbork Castle

The Teutonic Knights built this brick castle in Poland in the 13th century. It became their headquarters in 1309 and many more buildings were added to it.

Did you know? This may be the biggest castle in the world when measured by the area of land it covers.

Forbidden City

This fortified complex was built in the 13th century in China as a home for the emperor. His permission was needed to enter or leave the city. It is surrounded by a moat and tall wall.

Did you know? It contains about 800 buildings.

Moscow Kremlin

Found in Russia, the Moscow Kremlin was built in the 12th century and expanded over many years. Its crenellated outer wall has 20 defensive towers along it.

Did you know? The wall surrounding the Kremlin is 1.6 miles (2.5 km) long.

Great Zimbabwe

This fortified city was the capital of the historical Kingdom of Zimbabwe. It was built by the Shona people starting in the 11th century.

Did you know? The strong stone walls of the buildings were built without using any mortar.

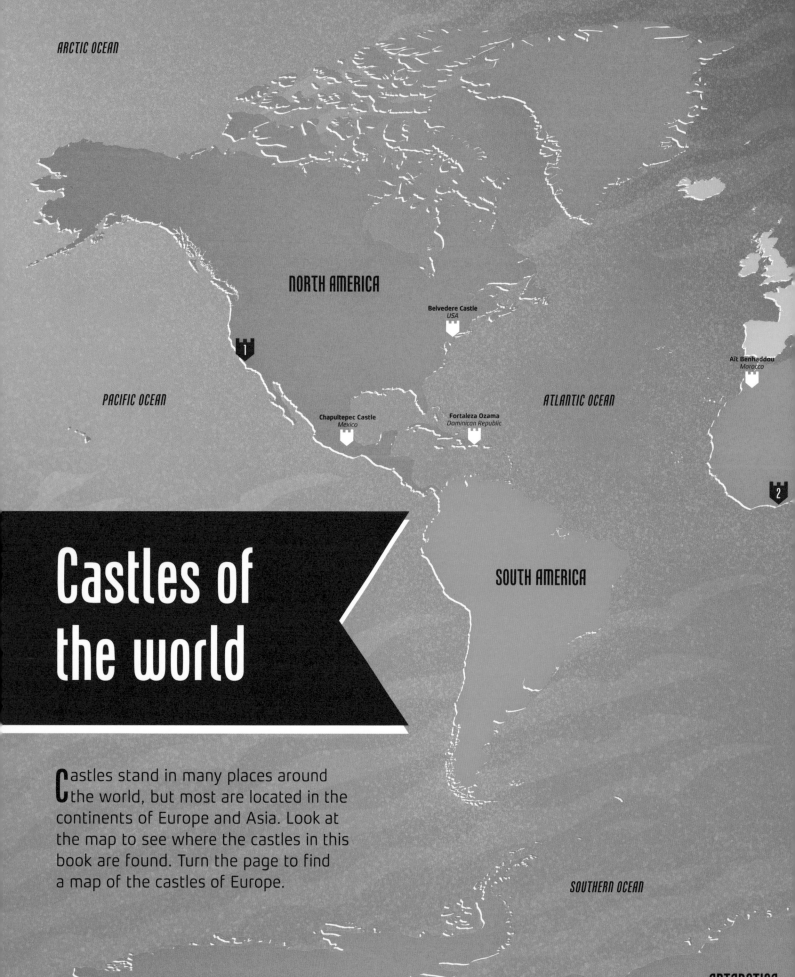

ARCTIC OCEAN

NORTH AMERICA

Belvedere Castle
USA

Aït Benhaddou
Morocco

PACIFIC OCEAN

ATLANTIC OCEAN

Chapultepec Castle
Mexico

Fortaleza Ozama
Dominican Republic

2

SOUTH AMERICA

Castles of the world

Castles stand in many places around the world, but most are located in the continents of Europe and Asia. Look at the map to see where the castles in this book are found. Turn the page to find a map of the castles of Europe.

SOUTHERN OCEAN

ANTARCTICA

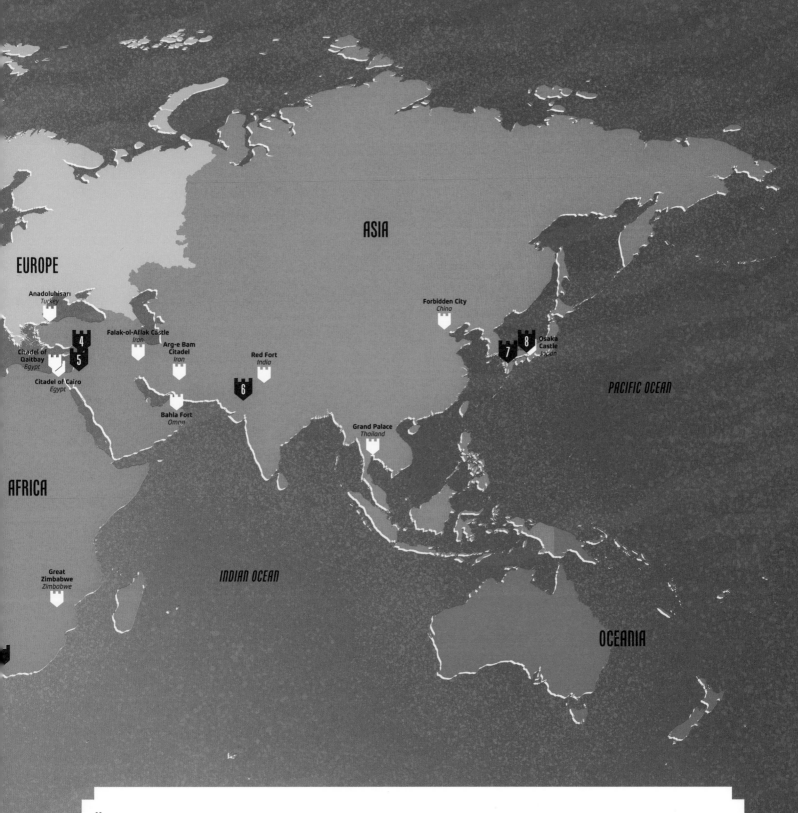

EUROPE

ASIA

AFRICA

Anadoluhisarı
Turkey

Falak-ol-Aflak Castle
Iran

Arg-e Bam
Citadel
Iran

Citadel of
Qaitbay
Egypt

Citadel of Cairo
Egypt

Bahla Fort
Oman

Red Fort
India

Forbidden City
China

Osaka
Castle
Japan

Grand Palace
Thailand

Great
Zimbabwe
Zimbabwe

INDIAN OCEAN

PACIFIC OCEAN

OCEANIA

Key

 1 **Hearst Castle**
USA
Pages 124–125

 **2** **Elmina Castle**
Ghana
Pages 80–81

 3 **Castle of Good Hope**
South Africa
Pages 114–115

 4 **Crac des Chevaliers**
Syria
Pages 40–41

 5 **Kerak Castle**
Jordan
Pages 18–19

 6 **Mehrangarh Fort**
India
Pages 96–97

 7 **Kumamoto Castle**
Japan
Pages 104–105

 8 **Himeji Castle**
Japan
Pages 120–121

ICELAND

Castles of Europe

Europe was a center for castle building in the Middle Ages. These fortresses were constructed, sometimes in less than a year, to protect vulnerable borders from invaders. This map shows you where to find the European castles included in this book.

Key

1 Beaumaris Castle
United Kingdom
Pages 48–49

2 Hen Domen
United Kingdom
Pages 8–9

3 Goodrich Castle
United Kingdom
Pages 74–75

4 Berkeley Castle
United Kingdom
Pages 84–85

5 Oxford Castle
United Kingdom
Pages 12–13

6 Southsea Castle
United Kingdom
Pages 66–67

7 Windsor Castle
United Kingdom
Pages 44–45

8 Bodiam Castle
United Kingdom
Pages 50–51

9 Château Gaillard
France
Pages 24–25

10 Château de Gisors
France
Pages 22–23

11 Carcassonne
France
Pages 30–31

12 Alhambra Palace
Spain
Pages 90–91

13 Chillon Castle
Switzerland
Pages 60–61

14 Heidelberg Castle
Germany
Pages 70–71

15 Hohenzollern Castle
Germany
Pages 102–103

16 Wartburg Castle
Germany
Pages 36–37

17 Neuschwanstein Castle
Germany
Pages 110–111

18 Scaligero Castle
Italy
Pages 88–89

19 Hohensalzburg Fortress
Austria
Pages 56–57

20 Predjama Castle
Slovenia
Pages 68–69

21 Bran Castle
Romania
Pages 54–55

NORWAY

SWEDEN

FINLAND

DENMARK

ESTONIA

LATVIA

LITHUANIA

RUSSIA (EUROPE)

Moscow Kremlin

Malbork Castle

RUSSIA (KALININGRAD)

BELARUS

POLAND

Czocha Castle

GERMANY

16

Prague Castle

14

CZECH REPUBLIC

Lichtenstein Castle

15

Burghausen Castle

UKRAINE

17

19

SLOVAKIA

MOLDOVA

XEMBOURG

AUSTRIA

Hochosterwitz Castle

HUNGARY

13

SWITZERLAND

LIECHTENSTEIN

21

20

SLOVENIA

ROMANIA

18

CROATIA

Srebrenik Fortress

SAN MARINO

BOSNIA AND HERZEGOVINA

SERBIA

MONACO

ITALY

MONTENEGRO

KOSOVO

BULGARIA

BLACK SEA

ALBANIA

NORTH MACEDONIA

TURKEY (EUROPE)

Castel Nuovo

GREECE

MALTA

Glossary

archeology

study of ancient or historical buildings and objects to learn about humans in the past. A scientist who studies archeology is called an archeologist

armor

hard, tough clothing worn to protect the body during a battle, usually made of metal or leather. A suit of armor can be made up of many pieces

artifact

object left behind by people from the past, perhaps dug up by an archeologist

bailey

outer courtyard surrounding the keep of a castle, contained within a wall

bailiff

person who worked for a noble to collect money and look after their lands, or an officer of a court of law

ballista

siege weapon made of wood and rope that worked like a giant crossbow to shoot stones or sharp bolts into the air

banquet

grand dinner, usually with lots of guests, often held to celebrate a big event

barbican

gateway or tower built over the path or entrance to a castle

bastion

extension of a castle wall, often pointed, that allowed defenders to shoot or fire weapons in all directions

battering ram

siege weapon made of a heavy wooden beam swung back and forth to knock down doors and walls

battlements

area at the top of a castle wall with openings to shoot or hurl weapons through

branding iron

long metal rod with a handle at one end and a stamp at the other, heated so it would burn and leave a mark

buckler

small, round shield worn or held on a soldier's forearm

calligraphy

decorative text written in beautiful handwriting

castle

well-defended and often impressive building or group of buildings, usually with walls and towers, constructed to protect people inside against an attack. Castles were homes to monarchs, nobles, the clergy, and other important people

cat

shelter used to protect soldiers attacking a castle wall. It could contain a device to claw a hole in the wall

Catholic

person belonging to the Roman Catholic Church, a branch of Christianity led by the Pope

chain mail

type of armor made from small metal rings linked together to form a mesh

chandler

craftsperson who makes candles from beeswax or animal fat

charge

heraldic symbol found on a coat of arms. Animals, plants, and mythical beasts are common charges

chemise wall

wall built around the bottom of a motte to improve its defenses

chivalry

code of rules that knights were expected to follow—for example, in behaving and treating others well and being loyal to their king or queen

cistern

pit to hold and store rainwater

citadel

castle or other well-defended building

clergy

leaders of a church, such as priests, nuns, or bishops

coat of arms

design, usually based around a shield shape, with symbols and colors used to identify a particular noble or knight

concentric castle

type of castle surrounded by more than one wall or moat, arranged in rings around the keep

crenel

open gap in a battlement for castle defenders to shoot through

crenellations
toothlike structures made of gaps, called crenels, and solid blocks, called merlons, at the top of a castle wall

Crusade
one of many military campaigns, in particular those waged by people from Christian countries to try and capture areas of the Middle East from Muslim countries from the 11th to the 13th century

curtain wall
tall, thick wall that circles a castle

daimyo
powerful noble and warrior in the Japanese feudal system

donjon
main tower built within the walls of a castle

drawbridge
bridge, often across a moat, that moves up or down to block the entrance to a castle and stop people from getting in

drum tower
round, drum-shaped tower usually built at the corner of two straight sections of wall

dub
make a person a knight with a tap on the shoulder with a sword

ducking stool
chair attached to the end of a pole. As a punishment, a person was placed in the chair while it was plunged into water

dungeon
secure underground prison that was difficult or impossible to escape from

excavation
digging something out of the ground at an archeological site, or a name for the dig site itself

feudal system
social structure where people work and fight for a ruler or noble and in return are given a place to live and protection from attack

flying bridge
bridge built on stilts to connect two parts of a castle securely

fort
strong building that is used for defense

fortified
made stronger, often by adding defenses or rebuilding in stronger materials

fortress
castle or other well-defended building

gallows
wooden frame used to hang people

gatehouse
building around the entrance to a castle, to keep out intruders

glacis
earth or stone slope that runs down from the base of a castle. Intruders climbing it must move slowly and are easy to spot

heraldry
practice of creating a coat of arms and keeping a family history, to identify someone

hill fort
ancient kind of fort made by digging ditches around the top of a hill to create protective walls and trenches

hoardings
wooden walls added to the top of battlements to protect defenders

inscription
words that are written down or carved into something

ishiotoshi
projections sticking out from a Japanese castle wall with holes in the floor, used for dropping rocks or boiling liquid down on intruders

jester
entertainer who tells jokes, pulls pranks, and clowns around to make people laugh

jousting
contest between two knights on horseback in which they ride toward each other and try to knock their opponent off their horse with a lance

kamon
Japanese design used to identify a particular noble, like a coat of arms, usually circular in shape

keep
main building at the center of a castle, often the safest place, and where the living quarters of a noble were found

knight
noble soldier in the Middle Ages who swore loyalty to a monarch or other noble and followed a set of rules called the code of chivalry

Knights Hospitaller
group of knights and soldiers who protected and cared for Christian travelers from the 11th century

Knights Templar
group of knights and soldiers who protected and cared for Christian travelers from the 12th century

lance
long polelike weapon with a pointed end, used in jousting

latrine
simple toilet, sometimes just a wooden seat with a hole in it over a pit

machicolations
projecting battlements at the top of castle walls with holes in the floor through which to drop missiles onto attackers

maharajah
Indian king

medieval
to do with the thousand years of history from the 6th to the 16th century, particularly in Europe; sometimes called the Middle Ages

melee
hand-to-hand fight, often between knights as part of a tournament

merlon
solid section on either side of a crenel (gap) in a crenellated wall

Middle Ages
time period in history from the 6th to the 16th century, particularly in Europe

minstrel
singer or musician who performed songs or poems to entertain people

moat
wide, deep trench dug around a castle, often filled with water, that prevented siege weapons being brought near the walls

monarch
king or queen

mosaic
picture or design created by arranging pieces of tile, stone, or glass

motte
hill, sometimes built by people, on which a keep was built

motte and bailey castle
type of castle made up of a keep sitting on a hill called a motte, surrounded by a large courtyard called a bailey

mural
painting made directly onto a wall, instead of on canvas or paper

murder hole
gap in the ceiling of a passageway used for dropping rocks or pouring boiling liquid onto intruders below

musha-gaeshi
stone slope that runs down from the base of a Japanese castle. Intruders climbing it must move slowly and are easy to spot

noble
person born into the upper class of a particular society. In the feudal system, nobles served a single ruler and were given lands in return

Normans
people who settled in Normandy, France, in the 10th century. The Normans became known for their powerful military

ordinary
shape used on the shield of a coat of arms to divide it up

organistrum
medieval musical instrument played by turning a handle and pressing keys

oubliette
kind of prison cell with an opening at the top and no way out

page
young boy training to be a squire and then a knight

palace
grand building, home to a monarch, noble, or important leader

palas
main building found in a German castle

palisade
defensive fence usually made of wooden slats stuck into the ground

peasant
farmer or worker who usually does not own land. In the feudal system, peasants belonged to the lowest social class

pentice
roof creating a covered walkway

pigment
material that gives a paint or dye its color

pillory
wooden frame with holes that held someone's head and hands, used as a form of punishment

plate armor
armor made from sheets of metal shaped to fit different parts of the body, such as the hands or chest

portcullis
heavy grate, often made of wood and iron, that could be lowered to shut off the entrance to a castle. A gatehouse may contain two portcullises between which invaders could be trapped

postern gate
small gate in a curtain wall, often used by castle residents to leave or enter without anyone noticing

pottage
thick stew or soup, popular in medieval times, made by cooking vegetables and grains together

projectile
object that is shot through the air, usually as a weapon

Protestant
person belonging to the Protestant branch of Christianity

quarterstaff
long, thick wooden pole used as a weapon

rack
torture device consisting of a table to which a victim is strapped and stretched by pulling their wrists and ankles

ramparts
walls of a castle, usually topped by a walkway

rebec
three-stringed instrument played with a bow, similar to a violin

rebellion
act of resisting the power of a government or leader

Roman
member of the ancient Roman Empire

sama
holes in the walls of a Japanese castle to shoot arrows or fire bullets through

samurai
noble warrior who served the rulers of Japan; equivalent to a European knight

scavenger's daughter
torture device that held a prisoner's body and squeezed it

scold's bridle
iron mask that wrapped around the head and stopped its wearer from talking; it was used as a punishment

shachihoko
mythical Japanese animal with a tiger's head and a fish's body, sometimes used in the design of castles

shell keep
type of keep with a circular stone wall built at the top of a motte, often used to replace an older wooden keep

shogun
powerful noble and warrior in the Japanese feudal system who was selected by the emperor

siege
act of surrounding a castle and cutting off its supplies so that the residents are forced to surrender

siege tower
wooden staircase on wheels that was rolled up to castle walls so attackers could get over them with ease

siege weapon
any of the different devices used to attack a castle, such as a catapult, ballista, or battering ram

slave
person held captive and forced to do work and regarded as property by their owner

slight
partly destroy a castle so it cannot be used again

spur castle
type of castle built on a spur—a high area of land surrounded by cliffs

squire
young man training to be a knight

star fort
type of fort built with pointed walls, often in a star shape, allowing defenders to shoot from every angle

sultan
Muslim king

tabor
small drum, often used by a pipe player to play a beat while piping

tatami mat
woven straw mat used as traditional Japanese flooring

tax
payment taken by an authority from its citizens

tenshukaku
keep in a Japanese castle

tincture
name for the colors used in heraldry

tournament
sporting competition where knights competed in different events, often lasting several days

tower
tall, narrow building, often forming part of the defenses of a castle

treason
crime of betraying one's leader, usually the king or queen

trebuchet
catapult-like weapon that uses a heavy weight to hurl a boulder or other projectile long distances

trench
long, narrow ditch dug in the ground

trencher
slice of bread used as a plate in medieval times

turret
small tower

ward
courtyard within a castle

zwinger
space between two castle walls, used to trap and kill enemies

Index

Acknowledgments

The publisher would like to thank the following people for their assistance in the preparation of this book: Caroline Hunt for proofreading; Hilary Bird for compiling the index; the staff at Bodiam Castle for providing information on the castle; Dr. Micaela Sinibaldi for providing information on Kerak Castle, with special reference to: *Bridge of Civilizations*, Chapter 8, by Dr. Micaela Sinibaldi, edited by Peter Edbury, Denys Pringle, and Balázs Major, Archaeopress Publishing, Oxford, 2019.

Picture Credits

The publisher would like to thank the following for their kind permission to reproduce their photographs:
(Key: a-above; b-below/bottom; c-center; f-far; l-left; r-right; t-top)

4 Alamy Stock Photo: Commission Air (tl). **4-5 Getty Images:** Universal Images Group / Prisma Bildagentur (b). **5 Alamy Stock Photo:** Boris Stroujko (cra). **6 Alamy Stock Photo:** Roger Coulam (tr); robertharding / Last Refuge (clb); David Lyons (bc); Chon Kit Leong (br). **7 Alamy Stock Photo:** imageBROKER / Jean-Yves Roure (br); Andy Guest (tl); Sean Pavone (crb). **8 Rheolwr Gwasanaethau Gwybodaeth:** The image AP2019_013_002 Hen Domen, Montgomery (C.651721) is Crown copyright and is reproduced with the permission of Royal Commission on the Ancient and Historical Monuments of Wales (RCAHMW), under delegated authority from The Keeper of Public Records. (bl). **10 Alamy Stock Photo:** Science Photo Library / Microgen Images (cr); Stuart Harrison Photography (tl). **Dorling Kindersley:** Natural History Museum, London (br). **11 Alamy Stock Photo:** Keith Morris (tr). **Dorling Kindersley:** Canterbury City Council, Museums and Galleries (cl, c). **12 Alamy Stock Photo:** Dave Pattison (bl). **16 Alamy Stock Photo:** Alexei Fateev (cl/crown). **Dorling Kindersley:** Courtesy of the Museum of London (bl); Combined Military Services Museum (CMSM) (cl); Order of the Black Prince (clb). **17 Alamy Stock Photo:** GL Archive (cra). **18 Alamy Stock Photo:** Jon Arnold Images Ltd (clb). **20 Alamy Stock Photo:** Steve Bentley (cb); Magdalena Bujak (crb). **21 Alamy Stock Photo:** Chronicle (tl); Tim Hill (clb); Mim Friday (cb). **22 Shutterstock.com:** Francois BOIZOT (bl). **24 Alamy Stock Photo:** Hervé Lenain (bl). **26 Getty Images:** Art Images / Merry Joseph Blondel (tl). **28 Dreamstime.com:** Grafvision (bl); Stanko07 (tc). **29 Dreamstime.com:** Filip Rasuo (tc). **31 Alamy Stock Photo:** dbimages (crb). **34 Dreamstime.com:** Anna Krivitskaia (br). **35 Alamy Stock Photo:** imageBROKER / Moritz Wolf (bl); Lebrecht Music & Arts (crb). **Dreamstime.com:** Viacheslav Baranov (ca). **36 Dreamstime.com:** Biathlonua (br). **37 Alamy Stock Photo:** North Wind Picture Archives (tc). **38 Alamy Stock Photo:** dpa picture alliance (tl, cra); Image Professionals GmbH / Walter Schmitz (bl). **39 Alamy Stock Photo:** dpa picture alliance / Jens Kalaene (tl); imageBROKER / hwo (br). **41 Alamy Stock Photo:** Anton Ivanov (crb). **42 Alamy Stock Photo:** Vladi Alon (c); The National Trust Photolibrary / Matthew Antrobus (tl). **42-43 Alamy Stock Photo:** Manor Photography (tc). **Dreamstime.com:** Grzegorz Kordus (bl). **43 Alamy Stock Photo:** Malcolm Fairman (br). **Dreamstime.com:** Arenaphotouk (tr). **45 Alamy Stock Photo:** Derek Croucher (crb). **46 Alamy Stock Photo:** Stanislav Halcin (tl); David Herraez (bl). **47 Alamy Stock Photo:** Norman Barrett (tr). **Getty Images:** Tim Graham Photo Library (tl, br). **49 Alamy Stock Photo:** imageBROKER (tr). **51 Alamy Stock Photo:** aerial-photos.com (tr). **52-53 123RF.com:** Gary Perkin (b). **53 Alamy Stock Photo:** The Print Collector / Heritage Images (cra). **55 Alamy Stock Photo:** Iosif Lucian Bolca (crb). **56 Alamy Stock Photo:** Gerd Harder (clb). **61 Alamy Stock Photo:** Alpineguide (crb). **62 Alamy Stock Photo:** Hemis / René Mattes (bl); imageBROKER / Stefan Huwiler (tr). **63 Alamy Stock Photo:** imageBROKER / Stefan Huwiler (br). **Dreamstime.com:** Stephane Debove (tl); Evgenii Iaroshevskii (cr). **64 Getty Images:** Science & Society Picture Library (cb). **64-65 Alamy Stock Photo:** Jozef Sedmak (cb). **65 123RF.com:** Adrian Wojcik (bl). **Alamy Stock Photo:** Jozef Sedmak (cla). **67 Alamy Stock Photo:** Vittorio Caramazza (tl). **68 Alamy Stock Photo:** Ana Flašker (clb). **71 Alamy Stock Photo:** imageBROKER (tr). **72 Alamy Stock Photo:** Richard Wong (cl). **Dreamstime.com:** German Sivov (bl). **72-73 Alamy Stock Photo:** Ernst Wrba (c). **73 Alamy Stock Photo:** Wayne J Grundy (bl); Nikreates (cr); Yuri Turkov (br). **75 Alamy Stock Photo:** funkyfood London - Paul Williams (bc). **79 Alamy Stock Photo:** Mim Friday (l). **80 Alamy Stock Photo:** Jake KY Anderson (bl). **82 Alamy Stock Photo:** Avalon / Construction Photography (tr); Chuck Bigger (tl); Sabena Jane Blackbird (bl). **83 Alamy Stock Photo:** DanitaDelimont.com / Alida Latham (br). **Getty Images:** The Image Bank / Merten Snijders (tr). **85 Alamy Stock Photo:** David Lyons (crb). **86 Dorling Kindersley:** Anthony Barton Collection (cla); Bate Collection (tr). **87 Alamy Stock Photo:** Ancient Art and Architecture (crb). **Dorling Kindersley:** Anthony Barton Collection (bl). **iStockphoto.com:** Stockbyte / Comstock (ca). **88 Alamy Stock Photo:** Peter Probst (tl). **90 Alamy Stock Photo:** Stefano Politi Markovina (bl). **92 Dreamstime.com:** Natalia Bratslavsky (tl); Joserpizarro (br). **93 123RF.com:** lachris77 (tl); Ivan Soto (tr). **94 Alamy Stock Photo:** Juan Aunion (crb). **Dorling Kindersley:** Warwick Castle, Warwick (cra). **95 Dorling Kindersley:** Robin Wigington, Arbour Antiques, Ltd., Stratford-upon-Avon (crb); Warwick Castle, Warwick (clb, br). **96 Alamy Stock Photo:** Tuul and Bruno Morandi (bl). **98 Alamy Stock Photo:** Rafael Katayama (tl); Zamzam Images (tr); Lucas Vallecillos (bl). **99 Alamy Stock Photo:** Tibor Bognar (br); Prashant Kumar (c). **101 Dreamstime.com:** Kuremo (crb). **103 Alamy Stock Photo:** Cro Magnon (bc). **105 Alamy Stock Photo:** Sean Pavone (crb). **108 Dorling Kindersley:** Board of Trustees of the Royal Armouries (tr/mace); Wallace Collection, London (l, tr, cra). **109 Dorling Kindersley:** Board of Trustees of the Royal Armouries (cla); Durham University Oriental Museum (tl, ca); Maidstone Museum and Bentliff Art Gallery (r). **110 Alamy Stock Photo:** imageBROKER (bl). **112 Alamy Stock Photo:** Norman Barrett (tl); Historic Collection (clb); Prisma by Dukas Presseagentur GmbH / Piumatti Sergio (br). **112-113 Alamy Stock Photo:** Norman Barrett (tc). **113 Alamy Stock Photo:** dpa picture alliance (crb). **115 Alamy Stock Photo:** Hoberman Collection (crb). **118 Alamy Stock Photo:** Stephen Finn (cla); Chon Kit Leong (bl); Prisma by Dukas Presseagentur GmbH / Van der Meer Rene (tr). **119 Alamy Stock Photo:** David Cooper (bl); imageBROKER / Peter Seyfferth (tr); Witold Skrypczak (br). **Dreamstime.com:** Petr Švec (cl). **121 Alamy Stock Photo:** Chris Willson (br). **122 Alamy Stock Photo:** agefotostock / I.S.G.M. (tr); Malcolm Fairman (br). **Dreamstime.com:** Narongcp (bl). **123 Alamy Stock Photo:** Af8Images - RF (br); Malcolm Fairman (tr). **125 Alamy Stock Photo:** Panoramic Images (cr). **126 Alamy Stock Photo:** aerial-photos.com (clb); Sulo Letta (ca). **Dreamstime.com:** Daliu80 (bc). **Getty Images:** The Image Bank / Tuul & Bruno Morandi (crb); Moment Unreleased / Henryk Sadura (tr). **127 Alamy Stock Photo:** Boris Stroujko (cla). **Dreamstime.com:** Anton Aleksenko (bl); Martin Mullen (tc); Paul Maguire (tr). **128 Alamy Stock Photo:** China Span / Keren Su (clb). **Dreamstime.com:** Blossfeldia (tr); Maksym Topchii (tl); Lachris77 (crb); Özgür Güvenç (bc). **129 123RF.com:** czekma13 (clb). **Alamy Stock Photo:** agefotostock / Anton Aleksenko (bc). **Dreamstime.com:** Jose Ramon Alvarez (ca); Megan Forbes (tc); Arapix / Nataliya Hora (crb). **130 123RF.com:** Sean Pavone (crb). **Alamy Stock Photo:** Iakov Filimonov (clb). **Dreamstime.com:** Natalya Erofeeva (ca); Hunterbliss (tl); Sangaku (tr); Rodrigolab (bc). **131 Alamy Stock Photo:** Banauke (cb); travellinglight (clb); Robert Preston Photography (br). **Dreamstime.com:** Dennis Dolkens (tr)

All other images © Dorling Kindersley
For further information see: www.dkimages.com